Ericka

MW00618371

WALKING

WITHOUT

MY

CANE

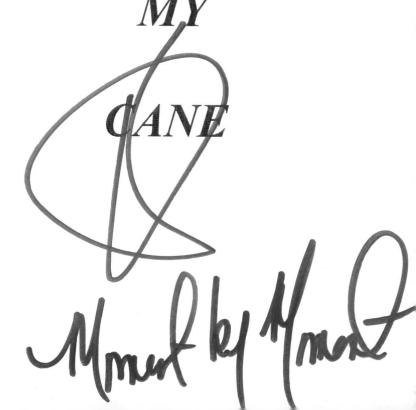

Moment by Moment

WALKING WITHOUT MY CANE

A Memoir Of Kimberly Nicole Johnson

DeLayne Publishers

Published by: DeLayne Publishers LLC
www.delaynepublishers.com

Walking Without My Cane by Kimberly N. Johnson
Cover by Elonzo Coppins
Photograph by Steven J. Edinburg

Copyright © 2017 by DeLayne Publishers LLC

All Scriptures quotations unless otherwise indicated are taken from the Holy Bible.

All rights reserved. No part of this book may be reproduced or transmitted in any form or by any means without written permission from the author.

Library of Congress: Cataloging-in-Publication Data is available upon request

ISBN: 978-0-9976180-3-7

Printed in the United States of America

Contents

Contents cont.

DEDICATION

This book is dedicated to "My Devan"; I will always love you, forever and completely. I miss you terribly. I will continue to live out loud like you would expect me to do until we see each other again my love. To my amazing sons, although your dad is in heaven, he expects you to continue to be the great men of GOD in which we raised. To my daughter N Loves, you are the girls we always wanted that GOD eventually blessed us with later on in life. To my grandchildren, you are Nana and Paw Paw's babies forever; I love you. This is only the beginning!

To one of the most amazing women I've been blessed to know, my mother Joyce L. Booker, GOD blessed us with each other. You introduced me to GOD from day one and I thank you for being my first love. I love you forever mom.

To my amazing "squad", I don't know who or where I would be on this journey without each one of you. We can't choose our "blood" family but we can pick our friends and they can certainly turn into family. You already know who you are; I will always love each of you to infinity. We are "framily" for life!

"GOD is good! Every day he wakes you up to do something productive with your life." -Devan Johnson

"I am free to soar. I was a bird in a cage for so long yet the door was always open and now I am outside the cage." - Kimberly Nicole Johnson

*Take a look inside the world of a woman rising and walking in her purpose after surviving some unpredictable events in her life, including unexpectedly losing her husband as she is learning how to "**WALK WITHOUT***

HER CANE!"

*Survivor: A. A person who does well with difficulties in their life. B. A person who continues to function or prosper despite opposition, hardship, or setbacks.

INTRODUCTION

Some days I wake up and I have clarity about what's happening in my life. Like today, it all seems to make sense regarding what it is I am supposed to do which is to share, inspire, motivate, and teach people about how life looks like after losing myself and my husband. This has been my purpose since I was conceived. I know this because my mom was in a very bad car accident when she was six weeks pregnant with me. She was thrown through the windshield and had over 100 stitches placed in her forehead after being in surgery for hours. The doctors told her she was going to lose her baby due to the bleeding.

Well, needless to say, here I stand at 46 years old as a survivor. That tells me that I have a purpose, as all who are created and placed in this world do. Are you fulfilled with where you are? Don't make GOD force you into your purpose the hard way. So many of us don't know what it is we are supposed to do and at the same time, so many of us do know but choose to ignore it. Being diagnosed at 43 years old with breast cancer and later on conquering it, gave me a new outlook on life, to live instead of just exist.

Losing my husband unexpectedly birthed a new version of Kimberly Nicole Johnson and it's shown me what real strength is. I never knew how strong I was until I had to "KNOW" how strong I was. My strength was already placed in me from conception so being a survivor was already a part of my DNA. Those trials were necessary for me to go through to become who I've blossomed into, which reminded me of how true and powerful the scriptures below are.

Jeremiah 29:11 *For I know the plans I have for you declares the Lord, plans to prosper you and not harm you,*

1

plans to give you hope and a future.

Psalm 139: 13-14 *For you created my inmost being; you knit me together in my mother's womb. I praise you because I am fearfully and wonderfully made; your works are wonderful, I know that full well.*

As I now think back to the weeks prior to this day, I remember how Devan and I were so happy and more in sync than we had ever been before. He was so peaceful and he would often talk about how he wanted to go to Egypt. The Thursday before his transition, Devan was sitting up front, waiting for his next client, looking out the window; it was apparent he was thinking, in deep reflection about something.

One of the ladies that worked in the salon walked over to him to say, "Hey Devan, what ya doing?" He said, "Hey E, I'm just sitting here thinking about my life, how thankful and grateful I am." He then began to name all of his blessings: "my wife, my children, my grandchildren... I've traveled the world doing what I love, our shop, our home...GOD has really blessed me.

I realize that I have done everything that I've ever wanted to do and the only thing left for me to do is go to Egypt." Who says that? A person who believes they will soon leave this Earth because they feel their purpose is complete. Was he saying Egypt because that meant 'Heaven" to him? My husband loved life, so for him to say that he's done everything that he ever wanted to do meant something more. He just had no idea how true those words were about to become.

I often say that my husband and I were one in the same. My husband and I would always finish each other sentences, laugh at the same things, and say the same things at separate times to other people unknowingly. So, it's of no surprise that I can feel him in my being and in my spirit. I was always silly, funny and blunt but I've noticed that it's even more so now. I can say something and laugh so hard at myself because it is 100% something I know Devan would say.

I am doing things now that my husband would spontaneously do. I have decided to step outside of what my regular life's routine was. Why wouldn't I do that? My life will never be the same, therefore how can I be the same. I have done more things for myself in the past 5 months than I ever have before. It is not that I couldn't do that before, but it was because I always put my husband (my cane) and family first. It wasn't that I was neglecting myself but simply focused on honoring my husband and family. So, I've decided that it's about Kimberly Nicole Johnson now and what I need to do with this gift of life.

~WALKING WITHOUT MY CANE~

I felt a piece of me leave my body on September 24, 2016, around 7:30 pm. That is the day my world was forever changed. I often ask GOD "Why didn't you allow me to sense something was wrong with my husband?" I used to be able to feel when something was going awry but on this day, everything seemed normal. We had an amazing time out the night before which was a blessing because it was rare that Devan was off early on a Friday. I'm grateful for that because GOD gave us that one last moment.

On Saturday morning, my husband woke up at 7:00 am like he normally did to start his morning routine. Before leaving, he came back upstairs to our bedroom. I was still half asleep when he kissed me. We hugged and said, "I love you" to each other and that we would see each other shortly.

That day I was going to a mentor training program that I now wish I would've never attended because I feel like being there took time away that I could have had to be with my husband. I arrived at the salon around 11:30 am. When I walked inside, it was loud and vibrant, full of laughter. I walked in and gave my husband a hug and a kiss. He turned his clippers off, laid them down, and grabbed and held me in a tight embrace to kiss me again. Devan knew that I would easily get embarrassed with that kind of display of affection but he didn't care. I had clients waiting for me so I went down the hall to start working. About two hours later, Devan had to leave to go see a client. He told me that he would be back in a few hours and we kissed again before he left.

The last time I saw my husband alive was at 5:15 in the evening. Our oldest son and his family came to the salon to visit like they always did, and our granddaughter asked: "Nana where's Paw Paw?" I told her that he would be back shortly and as soon as I said those words, he literally walked down the hall. He came back to the salon after being over one of his Celebrity client's house, preparing him for an upcoming event.

He gave me a hug and kiss, told me about his day, and then told me he was going to go home until I was done working. He kissed and hugged me again and said "I will be back. I'm going home to take a dump." You would have to know my husband to understand this. He hugged our oldest granddaughter, our second oldest grandson, kissed our oldest son, hugged and kissed our daughter and told me to call him when I finished with my clients. He walked up the hallway for the very last time and then he hopped on his bike. The next time I saw my husband he was lying in the street next to his bike.

That particular day was different because I hadn't had a busy day like that for months due to all of the breast cancer dynamics the year before plus I'd just finished the last surgery in June, which was closure for good. I surprisingly had a busy day and my husband was so proud of me because I was finally getting back into the groove of things. I often wonder if I didn't work that day, would things be different because I would've been with him and maybe he wouldn't have been on his bike.

After I finished my clients, I called my husband at 6:38 pm and there was no answer, which wasn't anything unusual if he was riding his bike. I straightened up the salon and dialed him again but still no answer. I figured he was riding his bike or maybe went home and fell asleep. Not once did I feel like anything was wrong with him. I had a quick stop to make before going home and in that moment, I thought "maybe I should ride by the house to see if he wants to ride with me", but since he didn't pick up again, I just decided to go ahead and make the stop first and then just call him again to meet him at the house.

After my quick errand, I tried calling him again but there was no answer but because I was close to home it didn't bother me. Devan always answered or returned my calls if he missed one. I just figured he was in the house, taking a nap or riding his bike and would call once he was able to stop. As I pulled up to my home at 7:15 pm or so, I didn't see his bike so then I knew he wasn't in the house asleep. I figured he was riding with the guys but thought to myself "he's going to get into a little trouble because he hasn't called me back yet."

I was about to park when I received a phone call from one of the barbers that worked in our shop. He never called me plus I just left the salon so "what could he possibly want?" I thought. I answered "Hello." He yelled into the phone "Kim something happened to Devan!" I responded "WHAT?" but he just kept saying "something happened to him" and told me to call this other guy. I hung up and quickly dialed the number that was given to me. After one ring, the guy immediately answered. I frantically asked, "where is my husband?" and he just kept saying over and over "Sis, Sis." I screamed, "WHERE IS MY HUSBAND!?!?!?!?!" ....

He wouldn't tell me so I hung up and I called Devan's brother Beng, praying that they would be together. I was frantic as I dialed and listened to the phone ringing. He answered and I asked him where my husband was. He said "Sis I don't know. I'm in Lexington, Kentucky." I began sobbing, trying to tell him what I just heard. He kept asking "what's wrong?" I told him "The barber just called me and said something happened to Devan." I gave him the number of the guy the barber told me to call so he could *call him and find out what was going on and I hung up. I then called each one of our sons and told them what I was just told. I said, "Something has happened to your dad." Not knowing what it was, they said: "we are on our way."*

I parked my car and went inside of my house. When the barber called me as I was pulling in front of my house, I was still sitting in the middle of the street. As I waited for my sons to come to our house, my heart skipped a beat because in that moment I realized what I was about to hear wasn't going to be good. As I walked in the house, into our living room, I started talking to GOD saying "GOD don't do this to me, to us. GOD, you don't operate this way." I started begging and pleading with GOD to allow my husband to pull up in front of our house. While I was pleading, I felt my body stiffen up. I couldn't move for a second and I had to shake my hands out so that I could move again.

In that moment, I felt a piece of me/my "soul" being ripped away from my body. I fell to the floor and I felt my husband leaving me, going to be with GOD. Our son Red arrived at the house first. He asked, "Ma, what's wrong?" I responded with "something has happened to your dad." I told him to call the number that was on my cell phone. As my son dialed the number, I sat on the stairs, rocking back and forth, praying and pleading again. I heard our son say "This is Devan's son. Where is my daddy?"

It was then that he was told the most devastating news our family ever heard. I saw our baby boy collapse to the ground and sob. Our worst fears were confirmed. I got up from the stairs and stepped outside where my son had fallen to ask, "Where's dad?" Red replied, "Mom, daddy gone?" "Gone? Where did he go?" I questioned. I couldn't digest those words that were coming out of my son's mouth.

Everything went black; I was wondering how this could be true because Devan was invincible to us or so we thought. I went into immediate shock. As we drove to where my husband was, we had no words. I felt like I was watching a movie. It felt like I floated outside of my body and was watching someone else's life. I could feel my husband over us, watching it all.

I didn't understand why GOD would want to break us a part. After all, he is the one who put us together. He gave us this life and this family. We still had so much to do with each other, including our children, grandchildren, family, and friends. It made no sense. GOD also knows how much we need each other and how much we mean to each other so I was still processing how this could be true. I guess it is my time to soar before I leave this world. Maybe the day that I asked GOD if there was more for me besides being a wife and mom, he was about to tell me "YES". God needs me to truly **Walk Without My Cane**.

~THE JOURNEY~

*The story of us started in 1996 when we met in Hair
School. I would always see Devan because he was really
close with one of our good friends. I was familiar with
seeing him in passing but also because he danced. I knew
him from that scene as well. I was a senior in hair school
with about 7 months left and he was new in school.*

*It was beginning of spring and on this particular day, I was
sitting in the dispensary which was something every student
had to do at some point. When someone worked the
dispensary, that meant you basically were passing out
things the student would need to complete their service on
the client. Devan came over to sit with me and we started
talking. After about 15 minutes, he got up and left. I always
thought he was handsome. After that day, I didn't see him
in school again. I later found out that he stopped going
because of his work schedule.*

*Some time passed but I saw him again in July or maybe it
was June. He was preparing to go to California to live out
his dancing career. We exchanged numbers that night. A
couple more months went by and one night I decided to
answer the phone. I had seen this unfamiliar number on my
caller ID box for weeks but because I didn't know the
number, I never answered it.*

*This night felt different so I picked up the call. It was
Devan. We literally talked on the phone for seven hours
straight into the next morning. I remember one of his
friends came over to his house and I heard him ask "Dev
who are you talking to?" Devan replied, "My future wife."
This man already knew we were supposed to be one. I was
taken aback somewhat because although he was super fine,
he wasn't my normal type but GOD saw differently.*

9

We quickly fell in love, was engaged 6 months later, and then got married on July 25, 1998, which was one year after he proposed to me while we were in Gatlinburg, Tennessee. I had no idea he was going to do that; yes, we talked about getting married but I didn't know that it would be that day that he would ask me to become Mrs. LaDevan Johnson. Of course, I said "yes."

Our wedding was something out of a magazine, beautifully amazing in every way and our bond was forever sealed in that moment. We drove to Atlanta and then flew to Cancun, Mexico for our honeymoon. We stayed for 10 days and it was so wonderful. That was the first time I flew on a plane and it was with my husband. We were a young couple with four boys, loving GOD, beginning our lives together and living the dream. We had no idea of the many journeys that would come along the way.

Devan and I always knew that we wanted our own salon and barbershop. From day one, we would talk for hours in our room after the children went to sleep about all the things we knew GOD was about to bless us with. Devan started barber school nine months after we were married which took 10 months to complete.

I worked in upscale day spas and Devan went to work in one of the best barber salons in Cincinnati, Ohio. After two years of that, we decided it was time to start working on our dream. I remember when Devan saw our first salon; we were in the car going down Gilbert Ave and we saw this "for rent" sign in the window of this building. Devan said, "Bae, let's stop and see what this is about." I was slightly skeptical but my husband always had a vision.

We stopped in and spoke with the owner of the building, and told him what we wanted to put inside because it was set up for an office space. I didn't think he was going to go for a salon going inside of his place but to our surprise, he said "sure, we would love to have your business inside." Wow! We knew at that point, GOD was doing this. We had the entire place renovated to accommodate a salon and barber shop and that was the birth of Incredible Creations Beauty and Barber Salon 2003.

Our salon Incredible Creations Beauty and Barber Salon catered to everyone you can think of from celebrities, sports figures, coaches, police chiefs, entertainers, moms, dads, and entrepreneurs. We became known as the salon/shop to visit when you came into town. Almost every entertainer came to Incredible Creations Beauty and Barber; we always wanted people to feel like family when they came and left. As we began to grow, I decided that just being a regular stylist wasn't enough for me. So, I became a platform artist which means "part educator, communicator, salesperson, and entertainer who performs on stage, mostly at industry trade shows, to promote styling techniques, tools or products."

Devan was very proud and supportive of that. He then followed suit and became a celebrity stylist and barber which was easy for him because we already had the connections and clientele. We both grew together and as the years passed, we out grew our space. One of my husband's clients came to us with a proposal to move our business to "OTR" which is downtown and at the time it wasn't a good place to even think about putting a business. We prayed about it and waited until God said "yes" and once he did, we started another salon.

We were the first black-owned husband and wife operated business in OTR. It was a major move for us being a part of the revitalization of OTR in Cincinnati, Ohio. My husband was a visionary and he saw things before they formed. Our

11

children were getting older at this point. It became clear to us that we were not just building this life for us but for them and their children. I've been told that Devan and I made people feel special, important, loved and accepted.

I must say we had some interesting dynamics throughout the years with people coming and going but we were still standing. When you leave out of our establishment, you left feeling pretty incredible, with a word from us, a lot of laughter, love, inspiration, connections and much more. We had people come by just to sit, laugh and talk. My husband and I worked hard to create Incredible Creations Beauty and Barber Salon; it was in our veins but only GOD knew how incredible we would become.

We knew we always had something special with each other. We would always say that I was the girl version of him and he was a guy version of me. That's how in sync we were together. My husband was my best friend after Jesus of course. We finished each other's sentences and we laughed hard at each other's jokes. I made him laugh and he made me laugh all the time. No matter what, neither one of us played about the other; we would slap the crap out of anyone that messed with either one of us.

Devan was invincible to me. I never put him to be bigger than GOD because I know that GOD is SOVEREIGN, A BIG GOD. Like all married couples, we had our ups and downs but one thing that stayed constant with us was our love and devotion to one another. We were tried but it just made us stronger. As I look back over all the things we went through, it was preparing us but mainly me.

~PURPOSE BEHIND THE PAIN~

This was the year it all began to change; the storm had begun when all of our staff left without telling us. One of Devan's clients told us that they were getting their own barber shop so we asked all of them separately if they were interested in that opportunity. Each one of them said. "No, we would never just leave y'all like that." I felt comfortable with what they told us but Devan was feeling something different.

They started to act different towards us, getting very cliquish, leaving Devan and me out of their mix which was suspiciously different since we used to be a shop family. So, one day Devan was riding on his bike and discovered the "new place" that we kept hearing about. He came home and said, "Bae, guess what I found out?" The guy has a barber shop just like we suspected. I said, well let's go pay them a visit to see if it's really true. We knocked on the door and lo and behold it was true. They really did have a barber shop which wasn't the issue, but the issue was that it was done in deceit. One of the barbers was inside his new barber shop that was about 90% complete.

Devan and I were heartbroken to some degree because we didn't understand the shadiness behind it all. Devan and I helped EVERYBODY we had opened our doors to every single person that ever came to work with us with open arms. We always had their backs but when they didn't like something that we would say or do then, we are the bad guys. So that is what started the storm of 2014 because we had no staff and it was all on us. BUT GOD!

Then a few weeks later one of our sons got into some legal trouble that our family had to deal with BUT GOD! Then my heart skipped a beat at 9:30 am Monday, April 7, 2014, which happened to be our oldest son's 27th birthday. My husband and I received news that would show us how precious life really is.

I was 43 years young overall healthy wife, mom, daughter, nana, sister, friend and entrepreneur, so how was it true that I had just been told that I had breast cancer? Let me back up for a quick moment, I always saw my gynecologist each year and did my own breast exams. I told the doctors that I felt a small knot two years prior but my mammograms always came back clean.

The year of 2014, I insisted that they focus in on what I knew I was feeling, so they called me back in after the initial exam about one week later for more testing. I wasn't worried to be honest because "people like me" don't get breast cancer or so I thought. I decided to call in that morning for the results again, already knowing what I would hear was going to be good.

"Hello this is Kimberly Johnson and I'm calling in for the results of the biopsy I had done last Tuesday." Oh, hi Kim, hold on for a second. Now, I must admit I sat on hold for about three to four minutes but it felt like 30-40 minutes. In that time, I knew what I was about to hear was going to be NOT what I wanted to hear. The nurse came back to the phone and said "Ok, so your results came back positive for wonk, wonk, wonk, Carcinoma! (That's not what she said but that's what I heard).

I knew Carcinoma meant Cancer. So, I said wait 'WHAT'!!!! Say that again……. My husband heard me from one level down in our house and ran upstairs as she was repeating herself. He looked at me in disbelief and I looked at him with the same feeling. I can hear the nurse saying, "You will be fine because it's in the early stage"

WHAT!!!! Because for me when I heard the "C" word, it meant you were dying within the next 24 hours.

My entire life flashed before me, I thought about how much life I still had to live with my husband; my children, grandbabies, mom, friends, and family. The nurse was very kind and understanding and we set an appointment for the very next day to see the surgeon. When I think back to that moment and remember seeing the look of fear in my husband's eyes it saddens me to this day.

I grabbed my husband's hands and looked him in his eyes and said, GOD, has this. We are going to win; it's done, and my husband prayed, hugged me and decided in that moment that we won. I'm not insinuating that we weren't nervous of the unknown because we were. We still didn't know anything about stages, types of diagnosis, surgeries, chemo, radiation we knew nothing until we saw one of the most amazing breast surgeons on the planet, which would become a dear friend.

Dr. Hilary Shapiro-Wright *was the first doctor that I met with of the amazing medical team. As I sat in the waiting room this woman, whom I never met approaches me and she asked me something that I felt at the time was invasive. She says, "Excuse me can I ask you a question? Are you saved?" I looked at her briefly then said, "YES" she then said, "Everything is going to be fine whatever happens you are going to be good at the end of it all.*

I looked at her as if she was crazy and then I thanked her. What was odd was that she was the only woman that didn't have on one of the pink capes that you wear when you get your mammograms done. When I looked back up, she had disappeared just like that she was gone. I told my husband what happened he too found it strange.

As I look back she was giving me a message from GOD that all was well and that I would be healed. Just go through the journey but I was going to be fine. We see the doctor and she gave us all of our answers on that visit, stage IIA, invasive ductal carcinoma/ with 3+ hormone receptors/HER2/Neu positive, no lymph node involvement, 2.1 cm (which is what made it a stage 2)

So, then it all begins test after test after test. A genetic testing was done which came back with no genetic history. I had MRI's, Pet scans, blood was drawn, a port inserted and much more, it was a very long road ahead. I went onto doing six rounds of chemo every 21 days with **Dr. Karen Dyehouse** which lasted four months April-August 2014, surgery in October 2014, which was an experience in itself.

October 15, 2014, was the day it was truly over, meaning that the hard part was. The surgery went well as we already knew it would. When I woke up in recovery my husband, mom, daughter, brother was right there. My son called us as I was waking up, which was from GOD because how would he know when to call me.

I woke up so thankful and very groggy. I stayed in recovery for a few hours, because they had to make sure I was okay before going to the room. My husband wanted me to eat but of course, I wasn't hungry and I certainly didn't want any hospital food. He made me order some food from a restaurant, which was down the street from the hospital. Before he left he made me promise not to get out of the bed without him, he didn't care if there were any nurses with me or not. So, I promised him I wouldn't.

He was gone for what felt like two minutes because he was back in the room instantly. As soon as he came back, I told him I had to use the bathroom so the little "PCA" was there and she seemed like she didn't want anything to do with me. So, I told her I needed to go to the bathroom and I sat up on the edge of the bed; walked into the bathroom all the while my husband is watching me from the other side of the bed. As I entered the bathroom I started to feel light-headed and I don't remember much else except my legs giving out and my husband leaping across the hospital bed and catching me. I believe if he had not done that, I probably would not be here.

When he caught me (after the lady allowed me to collapse with no help from her) his arms went around the incision I had from the surgery earlier that day. He put me back on the bed at that point all the doctors started running in the room. I said, "Husband I'm scared" because I felt like I was about to die. He said, "Bae, what's wrong? What are you feeling?" I then started throwing up.

The on-call doctor laid me down, checked me, and noticed I was bleeding from the inside. This meant that I was going back into surgery; regardless of just having surgery eight hours prior. I was scared and so was my husband but we both tried to be strong for each other. As we prayed about what was happening in that moment I felt peace. I said, GOD, we trust you!

As I was laying on the bed to go back into surgery, my husband was walking beside me holding my hand trying to be brave. We kissed but as the bed rolled past him I saw him smile and then when he thought he was out of my sight I saw him slide down the wall tears dropping talking to GOD. That hurt me to this day, knowing that he was feeling this pain, while I was back in surgery.

When I woke up he was right there sliding my ring back on my finger, kissing me, smiling, and thanking GOD the

17

whole time. So, did GOD hear his prayer not to let his wife die but didn't hear mine? I know that I have so much purpose in this life; nothing will ever make me believe otherwise.

*I then went on to have 25 radiation sessions with **Dr. Elizabeth Levick Dec-Jan 2015**. The radiation was decided on after the surgery; because a small tiny mm speck was found on one of the two lymph nodes that were removed, and after much prayer, and talks with my team, we said Ok. I am glad I moved ahead with it because I would've never wanted to look back and say, "What if."*

Tamoxifen will be my friend for the next eight out of the 10 years. I had reconstruction surgery June 2016, finally completing the long journey of Breast Cancer which has no face, no gender preference (although more common for a woman), no age, no demographic, no religion, or race attached to it. Breast Cancer (BC) can happen to ANYONE. My thoughts were GOD I don't drink, smoke or do anything to my body that I shouldn't do. None of that means a thing because that isn't the cause of Breast Cancer.

I've asked GOD what he wants me to do with what I've walked through, overcome and won. I know that it's more to the journey besides having it, getting cured, and just moving on with my life like nothing happened. I now have a story to share with others and I don't mind. GOD healed me and he handpicked the right team of doctors for the assignment.

I've had a total of three surgeries; lost my hair which grew back better, lost my fingernails which are now stronger, and I lost the only breasts I'd ever known for 44 years, which have been replaced with implants (love them) but one thing I never lost was my Faith in GOD!

It has been three years and counting of being cancer free. I have a personal trainer, I eat better, I keep stress to an all-time LOW and I'm excited about my "New Normal." The devil tried for decades to tear apart what GOD was doing, but he has no authority he can't curse what's already been blessed.

Now imagine overcoming all of this to turn around and lose my husband; after the journey, we went through in my life......

~NOW WHAT~

 On September 25, 2016, I wake up and I was in the guest room over my sister and brother's house. I'm looking for my husband because I can't wait to tell him about this damn nightmare I just had. I walk out the room and I see Stacey lying on the sofa and as she gets up to walk towards me and it all hits me that last night wasn't a nightmare it was my reality. I'm in shock, I'm spinning, what do I do now? Now what? It's all coming back to me Devan, My Devan is with me only in spirit. What about me? Devan, why did you leave me here alone? I just saw you and you said you were going home. Did you go home? Why didn't you stay there until I got there? What were you going to do? Why didn't you have on your helmet? Why this, why that!! WHYYYYYYYYY?

We promised one another that we would never leave each other alone. Why did you break our code? Did GOD need you more than I do? Devan, I need you!!!!! Please ask GOD if you can come back to me to us. You want me to do this without my partner? This life was made for the both of us, now it's just me. Stacey is right here with me and I know she will not leave me ever but she isn't you. She told me about the promise she gave you the night after you transitioned. She said, "Sis, Devan came to me in my dream, I woke up and he was standing at the foot of my bed. He had on all white linen with a bright golden glow around him." He was smiling, he touched my foot then said: "Sis, I need you to promise to take care of my wife, she is your sister, right? Yes, brother, she is. Okay stay with her always, I promise I will Devan."

~THE END AND THE BEGINNING~

October 4, 2016, today is the day we will celebrate the life of Mr. Devan Rmoni Johnson. I am actually going to bury my 43 years young husband whom I was with for over 20 years. My children will see their dad in his physical form for the last time today. I will touch my husband's face for the last time, our grandchildren will never get to sit on paw paw lap ever again this is it. I am in a daze, fog and I can hear everyone downstairs as they are getting dressed.

Our children, grandchildren, my mom, aunt, my brother, and friends are all here as well. I am upstairs getting dressed alone and I need this time to myself so that I can tell GOD I am ready to wake-up from this dream because I know this is not my real-life. The cars are on the way to pick us up and take us to the church. As I come down the stairs, everyone goes silent and looks at me. I smile as I look at my babies and grandchildren. I can see the pain in their eyes; they're trying to be strong for me, as I'm trying to be strong for them as well as myself.

The cars arrive for us, one Mercedes truck for me, our boys and my mom. Another one for our daughters and grandchildren. As we ride to the church everyone is silent, our stomachs are in knots because the reality is that we are going to see my husband in a casket. The man who was everything to us; the man we just saw 10 days prior alive and well, the man who kissed me on 9-24-16 and said: "I love you, call me when you get done with your clients."

He was the man that I grew with, the father of our children, the paw paw to our grandchildren, and the man that meant the most to me under Jesus. I look at my children and the pain I know they're feeling is more intense than my own pain for myself. They're about to watch their hero lay in a

21

casket. Please tell me that I'm dreaming. Please let me wake up from this nightmare.

We arrive at the church 30 minutes prior to everyone else because the cars were late picking us up. Our son Ryan was late arriving and I'm clearly in a daze. I see people standing around looking, watching all of us to see what we are going to do. I have given strict orders, "NO PHONES, NO PICTURES" I will not allow my husband to float around on any social media to be a spectacle.

My family and I walked down to get the first view before everyone else came in. I can hear my children sobbing, I can hear my grandbabies saying, "paw paw, wake up," telling people to let him sleep and not to wake him up." This is all too much for me to deal with. My children were so, so, so heartbroken and I see them sitting there stunned. Ryan our middle son is numb, he sat in the front row not moving just looking at his daddy. Antwaun our 1st born and Maurez our 3rd son stand next to the casket as people began to come inside.

*Again we didn't allow any footage so they're also making sure people honor that. Carmen, Stacey, and many other girlfriends are with me each step. They are fielding people away from me, I go back in the green room because it's TOO MUCH right now. I am having a service for my 43-year-old husband... how GOD, better yet why???????
My husband had over 2000 people attend his service. We had to extend the viewing hours to allow people to see him.*

Wow, I never knew this many people loved my husband it was like the president passed away. He was given a proclamation which means October 4 will forever be Devan Johnson Day! We had famous comedians, celebrities, city council, former Mayor just to name a few in attendance. The love we received from our city was amazing. We had people who flew in, drove from other cities just to attend and pay their respect to my husband.

As I sat through that service I was in awe. It was so beautiful how much my husband was loved. My sons and I had to speak at the service about this amazing man that GOD blessed us with. As I walked to the stage I could hear a pin drop. How could I allow my husband to leave this place without me telling the world what he means to us? I've had people say to me "You spoke at your husband service?" Yes, Mrs. Kimberly Nicole Johnson spoke at Mr. Ladevan Rmoni Johnson home going.

I don't even really remember everything I said because I asked the Holy Spirit to help me. However; what I do know is at that moment I instantly knew I was forever changed. I knew that a part of Kimberly was going with Devan and had already left with him the day, as he left this world. I also knew that this moment birthed the "Beginning" of me walking into my created purpose, talking on stages, yet it was the "End" of what I knew my life to be.

After the service, we didn't have the traditional police escorts, we had an amazing bike escort to take us to the cemetery. We released 43 red and black balloons. I released one gold balloon and my husband wouldn't have had it any other way. At this point, I'm operating off fumes and The Holy Spirit as we leave to go to the repast. We walked inside and it was like a surprise birthday party or a wedding reception. Yet I am without my better half and my soulmate.

The love in the place was beautiful. I stayed for about two hours I tried to greet and talk with everyone. I don't even remember how many people were there, but I do know there was so much love in attendance. I needed to leave and it was time to go home. The home that I shared with my

23

husband; to the bed, I never slept in without him unless he was traveling and to the only home our grandchildren ever knew. It's really real, my husband will never be in this space again. My children followed us home to make sure that I was okay. As I walked back up the same steps that I walked down almost 12 hours earlier and I am numb. I know my husband is about to call me and say "Bae, I'm on my way home" and I am going to wait for the call.

My mom is in the spare bedroom asleep and I am laying in my bed, our bed. As my phone lights up, I don't want to answer any calls, I just want to lay here and pray. I can't fall asleep, GOD how will I ever sleep again? God, I thought you loved me? Didn't you put us together? Were you mad at us? Did we do something wrong? Why did you separate us?

My husband would always tell me that I should write a book and I would blow it off. As I was walking to my seat at the service my cousin stopped to hug me and he said, "Cousin you have a book inside of you." I said, Devan used to always tell me that and he said: "I'm just delivering a message." Then it was spoken over me again soon after my husband's service. I hear you, GOD. I just buried my 43 years young husband, how is this correct? This makes no sense at all! So now what?

October 8, 2016, our second oldest son Ryan turns 26 years old today and his dad, my husband isn't here to see it. He passed away 14 days ago and I am still numb...I can't stop saying and thinking that I had to bury my 43-year-old husband. I was married to him for 18 years and together for over 20 years. I am missing him more than anything. I've prayed and asked GOD to give him back but I know that will never happen.

Unless I wake up from this nightmare, I can't imagine my

entire life without him. Everyone keeps saying "you're strong," really am I? Devan is me and I am him, which means we are one. So, if we are one and he has passed on that means a part of me has been removed. Correct? I can feel my insides being etched. I'm not sure what the writing is just yet, but I know that I will be changed forever.

I must admit I'm afraid and I asked for strength, peace, courage, understanding, and acceptance. I want to be strong and happy. I know without a shadow of any doubt that my husband, Devan would not want me to be sad at all. Devan would not want me stressed out. So, I focus on being happy in the moment.

This has truly shown me that life is short and time is precious. We all seem to take it for granted. My husband's passing has really inspired me and so many others to live out loud. I would've never thought this would be my life. Devan and I had so many plans for us, our family and friends. Devan was a one of a kind and very special man and he can never be replaced.

Our bond was so organic, natural and authentic. It's something that came easily to us and we never tried to be anyone other than us. I am ready to tell my story............My story is a big deal. I initially thought it was just about the Breast Cancer journey, but I've come to realize it's about Devan and me, the journey and being a widow at 46-years-old.

October 11, 2016, is the first day that I have been alone, with no one here at my home. My mom had to go back to work on Monday. My friend has been here since Monday, but she comes about 7:30 pm-8 pm and we chat before she goes down to bed. Another friend came over before she left and when I woke up she was already here. But today no one is here…I'm all alone!!!!! It's just me and Ava (my dog) and GOD.

I woke up and prayed for my peace, my strength, my courage, my acceptance, my wisdom, my discernment, and my prosperity. I also pray that nothing is broken and nothing is missing. I must admit that I have been having a little trouble with this one, no not a little, but a lot. Devan and I have always believed and received, "Nothing broken, nothing missing."

We also believed that we would grow old together, at least 120 years old. The Bible states: ask and you shall receive, Matthew 7:7-8, yet my husband isn't here. I know that to be absent from the body is to be present with the LORD if you believe in the finished works of Jesus. So I'm continuing to trust GOD because he doesn't do anything bad in our lives…………………GOD gave Devan to me.

I know he knows how important Devan is to me, so for GOD to take him back I assume means I'm going to be okay. I know for a fact my husband never wanted me to be sad, stressed, struggling, or worried. I know that GOD knows this and feels the same way. I can feel my husband and I also feel GOD'S favor working in and on my life, my children's lives, family, and friends.

~TALKING TO GOD~

GOD, I really, really, really miss my husband Devan Rmoni Johnson and I'm still processing it all. I have moments when I'm okay, then other moments when I'm not. My husband has been with GOD for 17 days. His home going service was seven days ago. It seems like it was just yesterday.

Meanwhile, everyone gets back to business, but I feel like the world was supposed to stop. How can everyone just continue like my husband didn't just leave the world? Am I the only one that feels lost without him? Am I the only one that doesn't know how I am supposed to continue on without him? I have never felt this type of pain.

I thought going thru "Breast Cancer" was painful and that GOD was mad at me. I thought seeing our two youngest sons locked up was painful, but this one right here............I just had a thought, what if my husband sacrificed his life for our granddaughter by praying for her life when she was born! I know that sounds like foolishness, but I can't help but wonder if that's true.

Just a few weeks earlier our youngest granddaughter was born six weeks early because she wasn't due until October. I went to the hospital with my son and daughter to see our baby come into the world. Devan was at work but told me to keep him posted and he would come over once she arrived. Everything went well but then she stopped breathing while they were cleaning her up. I heard our son ask the nurse several times if she was breathing. When I looked over at her she was blue.

I walked past everyone tending to our grandbaby went in the hall and in that moment, I called my husband. He was

27

working on a client and as I started telling him what was going on, he stopped working and started praying for our grandbaby. After he finished, I walked back inside the room and she was crying! I know GOD heard him because she is healthy and blessed. I guess I'm trying to make sense of this part of my life because I know that GOD doesn't play bargaining tactics.

I think of my husband all day every day. I've come to accept that he is not coming back physically. I know that he is with us spiritually. I know for a fact that Devan is proud of me and wants me to continue living. So, I'm trying to honor that or maybe I should say I WILL honor that. I know this too shall pass and it will get better as time goes by.

October 13, 2016, it's 11:30 pm and I just got in bed today. It was actually a good day and I woke up full of peace. My family came over, we had lunch and fellowship. I later met the girls for dinner at J. Alexanders, which was my first night out since Devan's passing. I had a fun night…….. However; the facts still remain the same, which is my husband isn't going to be home when I walk back in the door.

I've been asked to speak at a "Cancer Event" on 10-23-16 and I feel like it will be the start of much more to come. Devan would be so proud of me for doing this. I was talking about doing something like this before he passed away. I realize that it's time to start helping other woman and men I know that I'm walking in my purpose. It's so hard to think too far in the future because I don't see it without my husband. We had so many plans…… I will continue everything we planned. I am working and building our brand. We have a salon manager and possible full staff, as well. I can certainly see GOD'S provisions for me, us.

Devan has set the bar extremely high and he also gave so many people motivation to live a full life.

October 16th, 2016, this Sunday I went to the cemetery with the kids. I really have a husband that is in Heaven, but the shell is at Spring Grove. I went to a concert last night with my Sister/Mentor. This was the first night out in public without my husband since the service. It felt like everyone was staring at me. I wonder what they were thinking. "Why is she out?"

I've only been to one concert without my husband. As I sat in my seat, all I could think about was Devan. I was trying very hard to be present and I kept waiting for my husband to call me and say, "Bae, where are you?" I'm at the house." The concert was bittersweet but I'm glad I went. I felt sad because that was something that Devan and I did all the time. So, I guess this is what it looks like moving forward.

Can't Sleep

October 17, 2016, I woke up three times last night. This is the first time that I woke up these many times since my husband went home to GOD. I wasn't scared... just knowing it's real.

~REALITY~

I went to the funeral home today to take care of the bill for Devan's service. Since I've decided to move I have started really seriously preparing my mind. I've never ever lived alone. I went from my mom's home at 19 years old, to move out with my son when he was two years old, then with my husband. I've never had to think of what I wanted my home to look like without Devan and I doing it together. These are just some of the things I now have to face and deal with.

My throat is trying to hurt, I believe it's from the weather changing or is it stress? I stayed home Sunday, Monday, and Tuesday night alone. I called my friend to come over tonight. I also got Devan's wedding ring back from the Jeweler it's so pretty. They sized it down to fit my finger and cleaned it up. It looks like it did the day I put it on his finger. This is the ring I gave him almost 19 years ago when we said our vows. We experienced every single one of our vows "for richer, for poorer, in sickness and health, to love and to cherish "till death do us part" which was the only way we would've ever parted.

Missing Him

I think about my husband all day, every day. I miss him so, so, so much. I think it's very important at this stage to stay away from anyone that's negative and not for me. My prayer every single day is for the Holy Spirit to comfort me and my seven children, eight grandkids, niece, nephews, mom, friends, and family. Also for the fruits of the spirit I know that I'm going to be fine I just have to walk it out moment by moment.

October 21, 2016, Phone calls and visits have slowed down

drastically. My kids didn't even call much today. I spoke with a couple of my children today, but that's it. I'm home alone again. I had to go handle business without my husband so my sister went with me today. I need to decide if I want to stay in our house. In this house, we raised our children and the only house our grandchildren know. I really miss my husband it's been 27 days since my husband has been with GOD. I am running the salon and working our IC brand. GOD has already begun allowing people to bless me with so many things and introduced me to people who have a purpose on this journey.

October 22, 2016, it has been 28 days since my husband went to be with GOD. I miss him each moment. I'm remembering moments when we would be in the salon-shop or anywhere and we would both just start praying and realize we just said the same prayer. Or if one of our friends needed advice from us we would offer the same wisdom separately, at different times not knowing we just gave the same advice that's how in sync we were. There are moments when I feel guilty for living without him but then I remember that he is happily at home. I also know that if I begged him to come back to me he would say, "Bae, I love you so much but it's good here, I can't." I know that I would lose if he had to choose between me and GOD. I wouldn't even ask such a thing.

October 23, 2016, today I spoke at the Cancer Awareness Day Party. I've decided to share my story, "our" story. It was awesome and well received. I'm excited about what GOD is doing. I felt sad at different times of the day which is probably going to be part of my life for a while. So, I need to begin adjusting to this new normal and start working out because this is going to help with the grieving. I am going to meet with Jamie a personal trainer; who is also a 17-year BC survivor, only GOD knew she and I would meet one day.

October 24, 2016, today is Monday and I slept better last night. I've decided to let the house go. So, I will plan to move late spring early summer. I can then begin to purge, downsize and sell some of our things. I told someone today that I have four options:

> *A: TRUST GOD*
> *B: TRUST GOD*
> *C: TRUST GOD*
> *D: ALL OF THE ABOVE*

When I think beyond now and my husband not being here, it gets scary and hard. So, I stay in this moment.

October 26, 2016, I decided to go to Bible study at my brother's church tonight. This man visiting basically confirmed what I've been previously told which was "It's something about you, you have a titanium spirit." It's very strong, powerful, good and positive. I was also told by another woman at the church that she sees prosperity, prayer, and favor all around me.

Earlier that day I met with my new trainer. I've decided that I need to take care of my whole self and she also said she felt a very positive strong spirit. She senses that I have good people in my life that are uplifting me. The Holy Spirit has shown me his comfort. I see it's all going to be worth it because GOD is moving, elevating, and transforming me. I'm so grateful.

October 27, 2016, today is our grandson Ryan Jr's birthday, he turns four years old. This is the second big event for us without my Devan. This year will probably be the hardest of many hard ones. We will experience our first year without him. Next is Thanksgiving, all of the girl's birthdays, grandchildren birthdays, Christmas, New Years and all the others in 2017. I have decided that I will be on stages across the globe telling my story. I know that there is a purpose behind all of this pain. I have decided that I will get up each day with purpose. I will take care of my complete self-daily and it's going to be very hard without my husband.

October 29th, 2016, waking up today I talked to GOD I went back to the salon and I attempted to do a client but couldn't do it. I had to leave because I'm not ready for such a task right now. I'm going to start this new normal of life and I don't know what it entails but I'm ready. I miss Devan I really miss him, I think of him every second of the day. I bought myself some roses today because my husband did that for me on a regular basis and I must continue that routine I can feel him around me constantly. My husband always made sure that I knew how much I was loved by him.

~NOVEMBER 3, 2016~

Lying in bed still awake and it's 1:48 am. Will I ever have a good night's rest again in this lifetime? That remains to be seen, I have decided that I will move from our home before 2017 is over which is going to be extremely hard. This is the home that GOD blessed us with; where we raised our children, and it's the only home our grandkids have known. We have so many memories and it's hard for me to think about living here without him. It's not meant for me, it was meant for us.

Monday and Tuesday were really hard for me but today was a better day. I didn't cry today. I almost cried, but I didn't. GOD is providing everything good for me and my family. I thank GOD for strengthening me I am learning how to be Kimberly Nicole Johnson. I am evolving and being elevated. I will always love and cherish Devan Rmoni Johnson.

GOD took Devan back and now it's just me and GOD. I've always put GOD first, or did I? Now I have no choice except to place GOD above everything else. I am walking by Faith my every need/ want is being met. I am going to be a Public Figure, Speaker, and Author. The question now becomes "what am I going to write about?" What am I going to share? I have asked the Holy Spirit to show that to me.

November 4, 2016, I woke up at 7:20 am, that's actually kind of long although I didn't get to sleep until 2:30 am. As I sit in this bed I look at pictures and videos of my husband. I keep thinking "GOD, why isn't he here with me?" Why do my children no longer have their dad physically here? He won't be able to see them get married; continue to grow up, he won't get to see our grandchildren go to prom, and get their license. Why can't my grandchildren get to see their nana and paw paw sitting in the audience when they graduate; go to college, and continue on with life? Why do other people get to grow old and happily ever after? Why do I have to travel this next leg of my life without the love of my life?

I asked GOD if I did something wrong is he mad at me? I hear GOD saying this to me right now "No daughter I'm not mad at you. I love you more than you will ever understand. I am not punishing you, I'm moving you." I keep hearing that there's purpose behind this pain and it's wonderful. So, I know that GOD loves me/us so much and he doesn't want us to hurt ever which equals purpose.

When I think too far in the future the pain is unbearable, realizing my husband will never physically look me in my eyes, hold me, laugh with me, laugh at me, make me laugh, pour into me, motivate me, inspire me, pray with me, pray for me, pray for us, pray for others, hug me, hug our children, kiss our grandchildren, kiss me, and talk for hours about our future. All the things that made us Devan and Kim, Mom and Daddy, Nana, Paw Paw and it saddens me and only The Holy Spirit can comfort me.

I don't know and may never ever know why GOD has my husband so early. I do know that GOD sees time different from how we see it. The sudden unexpected passing of a man who lived every second of his life full and never took it for granted. He has touched so many people. He inspires me to live out loud and not be afraid "Though I walk through the valley of the shadow of death, I will fear no evil, for thou art with me, thy rod and thy staff comfort me."

November 7, 2016, forty-three days since my husband has been with GOD and it's 5:27 am and I've been awake since

35

4 am. I'm not sure if it's because the time went back but I woke up early yesterday as well, I was already waking up at 7 am now this. How long will this go on? I think I will try a hot bath tonight and tea. I am trying to tap into my feelings, my emotions, thoughts in this very moment and I wish I could go back to sleep. Sometimes, I feel like I'm in a bubble as though I'm out of touch with reality and time. I am starting to see who is for me and who isn't. Calls and text have really stopped from some and it's showing me who will walk this with me. GOD has to remove those not equipped and as long as he's doing it, it's okay. What he has is amazingly awesome, so I receive it.

November 17, 2016, have you ever heard anyone say, "Anything worth getting takes hard work?" I heard people say this a lot, what does this mean to you? I am on a flight to Las Vegas with my sisters and cousin. This was the last out of town trip my husband and I took which was just 4 months ago. I'm listening to "Blessing me" God I'm here, I'm listening to you father. I'm hurting yet, I Trust you. I'm so grateful for my sisters Father GOD please comfort me right now I need you right now. You are with me in this life I surrender GOD because I won't lose.

I want to keep asking GOD why. Why did you take Devan from me? I know that I may never understand in this life but I do understand its purpose. So, in the meantime, I just surrender to you. I am not alone and I know that. I was blessed to feel this kind of love from a man. I was a little girl that grew up without her daddy and had her first child at 16 years old. Yet still graduated at 17 years old and never went to night school or summer school. I was raised by a single mom that had a great job and blessed me with just about anything I ever wanted.

November 19, 2016, today is my second day waking up in Las Vegas with my sisters and not my husband. I was just here for a week with him, GOD gave us that blessing of time. It's funny because when we came back once again some of the staff left, so we were in the middle of staffing the salon. I am truly in this world without this man. When I look in the mirror at myself I see a new woman. I really do like who I see evolving, who is this woman surfacing?

NOVEMBER 24, 2016, First Thanksgiving without my husband and I was awakened at 6:06 am to the smell of food cooking. My mom spent the night and this reminds me of being a young girl living at home waiting for our family to come over for dinner. But something is missing and will forever be missing. "My Devan" I am in so much pain I don't want to get up today but I am because what choice do I have? Our house is full of love mixed with sadness. Although we will press through, we will acknowledge Devan. I can hear my grandchildren in his "man cave" talking about their paw paw. I don't think that they fully understand what it means to be in heaven all they know is their paw paw isn't here. It feels good to have my family with me but it just doesn't feel the same without Devan.

This was one of his favorite holidays. He would go to the shop and work until the end of the day. I wouldn't allow anyone to start eating until he came home which was typically after five. I would hear "mom we're hungry." Oh well, I mean no one ate until my King came home. Holidays will always be different for us. I used to love the holidays before this new world I've been thrust into.

I'm sitting at 1215 Wine and Coffee bar and it's the day after Thanksgiving. The first one since my husband passed away and it was very emotional yesterday. I'm feeling some type of way, missing this man so BADLY and I have to walk in it... I have no other options.... But I can say that I have been learning some new things about me:

I have discovered a strength that I don't think I knew existed inside of me, yet my husband knew, and he always spoke of it. I knew and know that I'm a strong woman but what I have been experiencing, walking in.... is a different kind of strength. I certainly know that it is The HOLY SPIRIT!! I have spoken about how I was my husband's co-pilot and I didn't mind one bit.

I'm not suggesting that I was unhappy being my husband's background singer, actually I enjoyed it. I knew that my husband was going to do what was needed to be done pertaining to life...his life, my life, and our life does that mean I was playing it safe????? Devan was my cane that I used every day.

I can feel my soul rising. I feel a newness inside of me. I feel like since my husband's passing has birthed something inside of me. I believe it's the Holy Spirit inside of me. I feel like I just want to be so much more authentically. Although, I thought I was living authentic before my love left this world.

But if I am honest I must say I did hold back at times because of honoring my husband and I will always honor that man... my man. He has given me a drive that I didn't know I had. I feel passionate about life...... I have never been by myself as an adult. This is a true definition of walking by faith and not by sight.

I believe GOD prepares us for our seasons before we enter into them and as I look back GOD was grooming me for this. I went through the breast cancer and healing me. The dynamics our sons went through, my husband being on the road traveling, me having to run the shop, and being home without him. The way GOD brought us closer than close. Devan and I discovered each other after the whole breast cancer issue. I'm thankful to GOD because I often say that he needs no help being GOD, so I know he prepared me for this.

I woke up at 2 am, 4 am, and 6 am; I just laid in bed quietly, spoke with GOD, and then drifted back off to sleep. I've found that when I do that GOD is waking me up for some reason. I was thinking about the conversation I had with my husband the Tuesday before his transition. I was sitting in the living room meditating, praying, and he came down with his usual happy self. He said, "Hey Babe what are you doing," I said, "I was praying, meditating, realizing and knowing that it's more to me than being just a wife and mother." I then said to him "don't get me wrong I love being those things but I know it's much more to me than that.

I know I didn't go through breast cancer, just to turn around and be the same Kim before cancer. Devan said to me, "Bae, you are already walking in your purpose and I'm so proud of you." He began speaking about all of the things I was beginning to walk in. I was giving a wellness event in the salon for Breast Cancer Awareness Month and he was saying how amazing I was. Was GOD speaking to me through my husband? My husband always poured into me and bragged about me, as I did him. I think back over this past year, Devan really was building me up. He had gotten frustrated with me two weeks prior to his passing because he wanted me to push myself. (Which I now know was a fear I had) I don't think I will ever feel this way about anyone ever again.

I don't understand how people say they don't believe in Soulmates. I believe GOD wants us all to feel what Devan and I have/had with each other. It was a oneness that can't even be put into words. I see what GOD has activated in me and now I have no choice but to act on it. The passion for hair is no longer there at this moment but the passion of being a mogul, owning my businesses that Devan and I started is still very much alive in me. I always felt everything that we went through was designed to try to break me:

Car accident 2001
Tried to attack our marriage
Tried to attack our finances
Tried to attack our children
Tried to attack health

Now my husband is gone……I am no longer a passenger of my life and I'm "Walking Without My Cane."

At this very moment I feel calm, relaxed, and at this very moment I feel peace. I also wish Devan was here with me. I now understand what he meant when he would say, "Bae, I need you to get it, I need you to know that you can do this." "I need you to see what I see" Devan would often ask me "What would you do if I wasn't here? I would say well I don't have to worry about that because you are here. Now as I think back on how I just took for granted that my husband and I would grow old together as one. But was I really taking it for granted? Why wouldn't I expect to grow old with him?

~WHY~

GOD, why is this my story? Why???? Why do you want me without my husband? Did I not listen to your call on my life fast enough? Did you have to take Devan from me to make me move? You saved me from so many things, like the truck accident in 2001. The enemy thought he had me cornered but you said NO! The breast cancer, you restored my family, and you prospered us just to name a few things. Yet you took my husband back. GOD, you created me and you created Devan for me but he's not here anymore. God, it's so very painful sometimes I feel like I can't breathe.

I feel so alone at times and when I look out and I see myself walking alone it gets scary. I know that you're with me so I'm never alone. Father GOD it just really hurts I can't even cry sometimes all I can do is moan. I surrender to you, GOD...... I wish I could see the purpose and the plan behind my husband and I being separated. GOD, you allowed us to spend every day together as one and now you want me to do this life without the love of my life. I don't understand but I've come to accept it because I know that you love me more than we love each other. Who do you want me to help? Who is this story for GOD?

I have moments of trying to understand why this is "My Reality" I keep coming up with the same answer which is......why can't it be you? If not you then who? I feel like it's a looming spirit of anger and rage trying to surface, is this part of the grieving process? I'm certain it isn't normal that I don't take any medicine to mask the pain because I need to walk through it. This time of year, doesn't feel like it used to. I used to love the holidays but as I sit here I don't feel that they will ever be the same. Everyone keeps saying GOD has another man for you. I want my man Devan.

November 28, 2016, Today I woke up around 7 am which is good for me considering my new reality and I did my praise and worship. I've decided to have a Tribute for Devan in January, honoring this amazing man. I'm in a very melancholy space right now, this truly is a painful process. We did everything together, I was my husband's co-pilot, VP, background singer, his first lady, biggest supporter, accomplice, and partner in everything. I had no problem being any of those things for him. I used to joke with him and say, "Husband I guess I'm your personal assistant" now GOD has moved me up in rank. Now I'm the pilot!

~MOMENT BY MOMENT~

As I sit here inside this coffee shop; I am thinking about my husband, as I do every second of the day. I will never stop saying, "Oh how I miss him." It's so very painful, it makes my stomach hurt. I realize that I am going through the different stages of grief. I have been teetering with "anger" and "rage." I look around and I watch as life goes on for everyone, not knowing what they may be going through. I wonder if they know what I am going through; what I am feeling, how much pain I'm in, how life is different for me now, and will forever be. I used to watch people peck away on their computers and I would often wonder to myself what are they doing? What are they tapping away about? Now, I'm that person tapping away.

When people ask me "How're you doing" I simply say "I am taking it moment by moment because that's all we have is this moment. I take no credit in what people see I also tell them, "It's GOD you see in me." I wouldn't be who or where I am without GOD. He is the reason I wake up and get out of bed, every day. I truly embrace each second that I have and I refuse to take life for granted. The day my husband was called home in one of his last snapchat post he said, "Every day GOD wakes you up to do something productive with your life." *Devan Johnson, my husband said that, so that's what I am doing. I'm not suggesting that we don't make future plans for our visions, goals, and dreams but not at the expense of living today.

My husband and I had plans to go see Kanye in concert that Sunday but he transitioned that Saturday. Which means enjoy "the moment!" The week of my husband's passing he told one of the ladies in our salon, "I was sitting here thinking how happy I am with my life and everything GOD has blessed me with: my wife, my children, my *business, and traveling around the world. I have done everything I've ever wanted to do; the only thing left is for me to go to Egypt." Who says that????? The Holy Spirit was preparing me for what GOD was about to do and I didn't even realize it in that moment. So, embrace where you are in the moment, live authentically, be true to who GOD has made you, walk in that, and give God the Glory in all things. If you aren't truly embracing your "TRUTH" you aren't truly living......and how sad would that be.*

~DECEMBER 1, 2016~

I cry every day for my husband and I don't know if that will ever change. Only GOD knows, yet I'm thankful for it all......

Today is another first we will celebrate without Devan this month holds a lot of birthdays for us. Today is two of our daughter's birthdays, followed by our oldest grandchild on 12-4-16. We were both there when she was born, she is turning 10 years old and no paw paw. Our youngest daughter and our oldest grandson's birthday is this month as well along with Christmas and New Year's Eve. This is going to be very hard for us nothing will ever be the same again.

December 2, 2016, Last night and today have been very emotional for me. I feel like I've been punched in the stomach. My husband is never coming home again. I'm not sure what stage of grief this is but I do know it's very painful. I pray for GOD to continue to heal my broken heart from losing my husband. My heart isn't literally broken but figuratively. GOD must know my strength better than me, well I know that he does because he created me. I feel sad, mad, angry, hurt, scared, alone, and I keep asking the same thing why, why, why? I have moments of being okay then the next I'm completely in tears.

It's been 69 days since my husband has been with GOD. I feel like some people look at me, feel sad, and sorry for me because they know what Devan and I shared. They truly feel my pain personally. I know that I am a strong Godfearing woman. I wonder if Devan knows that I am sad. I wonder what he's doing right now. I wonder if he's proud of me/us. GOD, please tell my husband how much I miss him, how much his children, grandchildren, friends 'aka' and family miss him. Please tell him I am walking in my purpose and I will not let you down or him. Can you tell him I understand why he was pushing me so much this year? GOD can you tell him that I will never forget him. GOD please give me peace right now and comfort me in this moment.

I've decided to go to Tampa for the New Year to visit Jules and Todd on December 28, 2016, and I will stay until Jan 4, 2017. This is a big deal because I've never ever flown alone and if my husband was here I would've never gone alone. I often wonder how my husband would've handled being left here without me. I guess he endured enough with the Breast Cancer ordeal and the surgeries. He was so strong and brave for me. Yet, I know that it "killed" him on the inside because he couldn't do anything to help me the way he wanted to. A lot of men would've walked out on their wife but not Devan, he was the best husband and example of a man to our children. Because of him, they know how to treat a woman.

I'm not answering calls from anyone tonight I'm taking this time to write and listen to music. This is something I need to do for me. I am in this big house all alone. I have my family and friends who would be here in a heartbeat if I called. But it won't fill the void that I have. I want to know if I will always feel like this. This realness is settling somewhat and it started to sink in on Thanksgiving Day and each day it gets more real. I can't sleep without him GOD please give me sleep. Will I always be awake like this? So many thoughts and questions.

December 5, 2016, I stayed home all day I'm just in the space to be alone. I laid around pretty much all day. Today may be the first day that I haven't cried. I've been dreaming about Devan but he isn't really speaking in the dreams. It's only me talking to him, he smiles but no words. What does that mean?

*AUTHENTIC - Authentic: not false or copied; genuine; real

I'm back at the coffee shop writing again. These past few weeks have been very emotional for me I believe the time is making it all so real. I am in this space and place of feeling everything that needs to be felt right now. I feel sad, yet excited about what's to come. I feel love and loved all at the same time in this very moment. I have been dreaming about my husband a lot more lately. In the dreams, I can't remember if he actually speaks to me but he is certainly always smiling, and that gives me peace and comfort.

I talk to him in all of them and I am always asking him something like "Why" or I may say, "I miss you." One of the dreams I told him "I miss hugging and kissing you" I also said, "I wish we could make love once more" he started smiling and said "We will have to hurry up" and then I awake to my reality...... Which is that my husband isn't here physically and never will be again.

People tell me that I am doing so well considering what has happened. I think to myself "Am I?" I must give credit where it belongs; GOD, GOD, and GOD!!!! He has also placed the most awesome circle around me during this time and season of my life. This season, I am walking in right now is showing me some amazing things about GOD and it's showing me some amazing things about me. The journey my husband and I walked "2014" was a storm that we already knew we would overcome because GOD told us at the beginning of it that "IT'S DONE!" We had so many plans afterwards for our future......but those were "our" plans...We can't get so caught in planning for the future that we don't enjoy the NOW! Devan and I always enjoyed

47

the now and we lived by the term "Moment by Moment" and "Just Be."

Losing my husband so suddenly and beating breast cancer has taught me to truly, truly stop; smell the roses, stop worrying about tomorrow, be AUTHENTIC, be honest, and live in your truth. My husband did all of the above while honoring GOD and always giving him the glory, loving his wife and family at the same time. This has inspired me to walk in my purpose and not be afraid of the "what" and follow the "who" which is GOD. Someone right now needs to hear what I have to say; someone just got diagnosed with something, someone just lost a loved one, and they have no clue how they will continue on in this life.

I have come to realize that this pain has a purpose, this pain will somewhat fade over time but will never be forgotten. This pain is attached to greatness and success, this pain is not designed to hurt it is designed to heal. It makes you search inside of the place you were scared to look because time is of the essence. People often say we only live once. I disagree we live each day that GOD wakes us up so in the words of my husband, "Every day that GOD wakes you up, do something productive with your life." *Devan Rmoni Johnson*

Feel, love, embrace, trust, say sorry, say how you truly feel, touch, be touched, laugh, cry, hug, talk, listen, dance, sing, eat, exercise, read, travel, teach, learn, and……LIVE!!!!! But most importantly…..PRAY, TRUST GOD, HAVE FAITH, know that there is nothing broken, and nothing missing as long as you're allowing GOD to lead you!

GOD, what is happening to me? I sometimes ask this question. I'm feeling peaceful in this very moment right now…..I'm also deeply missing my husband right now as well. It's cold outside and this will be my first of many winters to come without Devan. I feel so free in this moment and I feel my husband being so deeply a part of me. I have always felt and been authentic but I really feel it now!!! Why is that GOD?

I feel like my shell has been removed almost like how a caterpillar turns into a butterfly. The butterfly has an exquisite beauty, as it comes into the new life of being a butterfly representing endurance, change, hope, power, and LIFE. This is what this journey is about and I have nothing to lose. I will live for GOD and myself because I have a purpose. I have no shackles, nothing holding me back. GOD has everything before me and all I have to do is walk forward and enjoy the journey!

December 8, 2016

Butterfly:
Time
Soul
Grace
Growth
Elegance
Lightness
Surrender
Transition
Expression
Celebration
Resurrection
Vulnerability

I went to get a tattoo which is what most people do when someone passes. I wanted another one after the breast cancer was behind us, but now it's not even about that, it's about why husband. Needless to say, I do not like it. I wanted a pink butterfly to represent beauty, transformation, strength, courage, coming into true self, and purpose rising above it all. Yet, it looks like a pink rose!

49

December 10, 2016, this very moment I am writing with my husband's engraved pen that was given to him, but he never used it. I noticed it sitting on his station, so I grabbed the box, opened it to find a beautiful pen and pencils. This was a sign that I am doing the correct thing with writing and sharing. How symbolic and special will they be for me moving forward because they belonged to my husband?

December 15, 2017, Right now I feel calm, relaxed and peaceful. Although I am yearning my husband, I can't help but think about what I would be doing if he was here. I would be in the house lying across the bed watching some mindless shows and he would be downstairs listening to music, writing, and working on his purpose and craft. I certainly wouldn't be walking in what I now know is my purpose at all. I would have felt like something was missing deep inside.

The week my husband passed away we were even more in sync. I was sitting in the salon up front close to him and I was just watching him clean his station off. I said, "Husband, I love you so much and I love how we are so into each other in every way. I told him how attracted I was to his mind, as well as him as a whole. He walked over to me gave me a quick kiss and said: "Thank you, baby, I love you too." I will never have this again with Devan. My brain is still processing the fact that he has vanished from this world. I'm just saying this man never really got sick or hurt, so to have a bike accident (which he knew how to ride) was shocking to me and to skip being hurt and go straight home to GOD is surreal. GOD gave us to each other and it's hard when I think about him not being with me.

We did so much in such a short time we use to talk about the fact that we did everything together so fast. If you would've read without knowing anything about us, you would've thought 60 years plus couple would walk in the room. I see how people look at me sometimes and I see a look of sadness for me, as well as sorrow. I understand some people don't know what to say to me so some say nothing.

December 19, 2016, something was missing inside of me, something unfulfilled and now I think I found it, but my husband isn't here so what does that mean? Tears are falling as I write these words. I never imagined my life without Devan after all we've been through and now he's gone. I often think about how things would've been for him without me in it. I wouldn't want Devan to feel this or my children, grandchildren, family, and friends. When I look at our sons my spirit feels so deeply for them because the man of their life is gone. I'm glad they have GOD and their faith is being made stronger, as well as their relationship with GOD.

December 20, 2016, I went to bed at 3:30 am, woke up at 7 am because today is our oldest grandson's birthday and he called his Nana. He is 9 years old and Paw Paw isn't here, GOD please help us. I am sitting in the tub as I write, soaking and thinking. I think working out with my trainer is helping me through this grief. It's an antidepressant for me. Today, I realized that I have stepped into a space of authenticity to the fullest which means truly feeling every second. Dancing like no one is looking, singing like I'm alone, giving love, being loved, and communicating how to JUST BE! Devan taught me so much about life and love and I am going to walk in it.

December 21, 2016, today was not a good day I stayed in bed all day. I just felt like it was that kind of day. I've cried off and on all day today. I would say that the Holy Spirit must've wanted me to stay home because I don't typically stay home on a weekday, especially in the bed. I like staying busy so I typically go out, but today was different. December 22, 2016, Eighty-Nine days since my world changed forever. Yesterday was up and down for me. I was alone and sat in pain. I prayed, worshiped, sat still, laughed out loud, cried, cried, cried, cried, and laid around. I guess this is all part of the walk of a widow. I woke up this morning watched our videos and broke down again. My son must've felt something was wrong with me because he called and texted me at 5:30 am checking on me. This reminded me of the dream he had a few days earlier. He dreamt that I took some pills and passed away because I couldn't take the pain of losing their dad. I know that GOD has his hands all over me and my family. I released some more this morning. I cried out to GOD and asked him what did I do? My family is broken, my children no longer have their dad, but I know GOD knows what he is doing.

People wonder how I am doing and what I'm going to do now moving forward. First thing is my faith and trust in GOD is phenomenally amazing. Secondly, I allow myself to feel whatever I need to feel and be in the moment. Third, I have the best "squad" in the world according to me. GOD handpicked each one.

December 24, 2016, First Christmas Eve without "My Devan" it doesn't even feel like it's a holiday which is fine with me. Our son Antwaun just left, he came over and stayed for a few hours in his dad's closet. He went through some of his things which was very hard for him. I love my children so much, they are truly their daddy's sons. All of our boys are so laid back, calm, chill, extremely funny, easy going, loving, and caring. I wish they still had their daddy here with them. They feel so lost without him. I can't tell them how to grieve because it's a personal experience.

I went to Victoria Secret today I bought two very cute bras and I realized how important it was for me to do that. Which made me further realize although my husband is gone I still need to take care of myself inside and out. When you've lost the love of your life; you're used to being told that you're pretty, beautiful, and having your spouse admire you.

That's another aspect of your life that is different for you. It's another part of grief that you will have to move through. You don't just mourn the person you mourn everything about them. The trip is four days away. I am nervous and excited all at the same time. I am going to Tampa for the first time. I already know this is the beginning of something amazing that GOD has for me.

December 25, 2016, today was a very emotional day for me. I attended church and hung out with my brother, I had a good time. We went to dinner and then to the movies which is exactly what Devan and I would've done. I'm thankful for my "squad" they are a big part of my life. I didn't want to have anything at the house because it wouldn't be the same. How can I carry on family traditions when a big piece of our family is gone? Moving forward we will have to established a new tradition for our family, I don't know what they will be; however, GOD knows and he is allowing all of this to be. So, we will "Just Be."

December 25, 2016   **Letter to Devan**

Dear Husband,
I miss you so so so much I know that you are in a much better place. I know that you are happy and with our Father, but I wish that you were here with me, our children, our daughters, babies, family, and friends. I have been waking up early because you aren't here. You always knew

53

I could never fully sleep in the house without you next to me. Husband I am trying to be strong because I know that's what you expect of me, yet it is so very hard. The Holy Spirit is my comforter and GOD is with me every step that I take. I am being taken good care of GOD is making sure of that.

Husband, I now understand why you were pushing me so hard all this year (2016) I believe the Holy Spirit was telling me through you that I was ready. Husband, do you remember the day we sat in the living room talking before going to work on that Tuesday before you went home? I said to you that I was feeling like it was more to me than just being a mom and a wife. I said that I loved being those things, but I felt like it was more to me than that. I said I think it's time for me to start telling my story. You looked at me and said, "Bae, you're already doing it, look at all those boxes in the kitchen for women, you are doing it, Bae," I cried, you hugged me, kissed me, and said I Love you. Now, let's go to work, we got people waiting.

When I think back over that entire week GOD knew that this would be our last week together physically and our week was amazing. I think back to that Wednesday or Thursday that we were inside the shop waiting for your clients and you were cleaning off your station and I was sitting there just watching you. I said husband I LOVE you, I LOVE how we are, and I LOVE how we can have good deep talks about anything. I then told you how I thought that was a turn on. I said, don't get me wrong you're certainly fine and all but I see past that. You laughed and said, 'I know what you mean Bae," and we enjoyed that moment.

You were sitting on the nail stool in the window talking on the phone and I came and stood in between your legs and hugged you. I had to move husband because I can't remember what you were eating, but whatever it was made me move. We laughed and I walked in the back. Devan, you are my best friend under Jesus of course and I just miss everything about you. We didn't make moves without each other so how am I supposed to do that now? I know I can do all things through Christ who strengthens me.

Husband, I am so hurt right now, so very hurt. However, your transition has given me a strength and drive that only GOD knew I had and I believe you knew it also. I'm going to be a motivational speaker for women and maybe I can motivate and inspire men as well. I am going to tell the story of us. Your children are hurting but I tell them to pull from what you have poured into them. I know you are proud of all of them, your grandbabies miss you so much they say, "Nana I wanna go with my paw paw" or they say, "Nana I don't want Paw Paw to be in heaven, I want him to be here with us." I say, "I know my babies but Paw Paw is aware and still with us."

December 26, 2017, Husband yesterday was Christmas, but you already know that. I imagined you in Heaven celebrating with Jesus because it's his birthday. I didn't do our family tradition of Christmas Eve with the kids because it wasn't going to be the same. I went to church with Brother Kevin and Sister April. It was hard for me and afterwards, I was going to go visit my mom and aunt Lit, but I just went home and laid down. Brother called me a couple hours later and I went to dinner and the movies with them, which was a nice time. Brother has been really great with making sure that I'm okay. You would be happy. I enjoy going to their church but you already know how that is because we use to go, every Thursday night for about two months straight.

I have been in the house all day today because I woke up at 4 am. I decided to just chill out and prepare for my trip to

Tampa in three more days. Husband, you would be so proud of me for traveling and flying alone. I was scared at first but I know that I won't be alone because The Holy Spirit is with me always. Guess what else, husband I got my passport remember we kept talking about getting ours because you wanted to take me to Canada. I had your ring sized to fit me and I wear it every day along with some of your bracelets and your pics are all around the house.

I cry for you EVERY, EVERY, and EVERY DAY!!!! The Holy Spirit comforts me in those moments also. You are so inside of me, it's amazing how much I can feel you. We always did act alike but I really act like the both of us now and I love it. I am running the business GOD is providing everything I am going to need moving forward and it's all so good husband. I am preparing your tribute event and I have an amazing group of people helping and it's all due to the love you gave them and they want to give back to you. According to 2 Peter 3:8 one day is like a thousand years, and a thousand years is like a day to GOD, so it isn't good bye.
~I will love you forever and ever~
Mrs. Kimberly Nicole Johnson

December 26, 2016

I watched Devan on the Gary Owen show and I lost it. I remember when he was there while they filmed the pilot. My husband was so proud of that show not only because he was going to be aired on it, but because he was proud of them having their own show. My husband was at their home hours before he passed away, helping with an upcoming event he was going to. I barely slept last night due to the pain of knowing my husband didn't get a chance to see it.

Devan promoted and talked about that show like it was his, he worked so hard for everything. He accomplished, he never took things or people for granted. Just try to imagine for a minute seeing your other half on the television screen, but you can't see them in reality. I literally remember the day they filmed that scene. I woke up early, as usual, went to the gym which helped me release some anger. Devan's tribute will be in the next few weeks which will open back up some wounds, but we must honor him. I am listening to music as I write to help soothe my soul. GOD will you please tell Devan that I miss him so much in Jesus name Amen.

My husband took care of me in every way and GOD will continue to make sure that it doesn't stop. GOD is providing for me. I came home to a check in my mailbox and a gift card so unexpected. I was told that it's just the beginning of how GOD is about to provide and it will be overflow. I receive all of that GOD.

December 28, 2016

Finalizing the event for Devan January 14, 2017

End of 2016

Well, today is December 29, 2016, and I am on a plane flying to Tampa to visit my Sister Julie along with my Lil sister Dani. Dani was coming on Saturday but Julie upgraded her flight so she could fly with me today. I am so blessed and highly favored which also means my squad is blessed as well. I'm not suggesting that it's only because I am so blessed; however, they will experience the blessings as well. This is my second trip without my husband not being in this world.

I am in a place of such peace and I've been awakened!!!!
This is amazing and scary to some extent, but I like it
because I am not alone at all. As I sit here and look out at
the clouds I wonder what my husband is doing. Is he proud
of me? Yes! Would he expect me to carry on and live? Yes!
When I think about him riding that bike that day I often
wonder what was going on in his mind did he realize at
some point that he was in trouble?

I remember when I had a truck accident and I saw myself
about to hit the wall and I heard my children and seen my
husband flash before me. In that moment, I called out to
Jesus and everything stopped. I wonder if he called out to
Jesus but because it was just his time anyway. GOD said
it's time to come on home son. Did I flash before his eyes?
Did our family come to his mind? Knowing my husband, he
thought he had everything under control. This is all so
foreign to me and when I say all, I mean all of this.........
no Devan and Kim, Nana and Paw Paw, Brother and
Sister, and Mom and Dad......... in the physical sense! I am
in discovery mode now self.

Who is Kimberly Nicole Johnson? Maybe I should first ask
who "was" Kimberly Nicole Johnson? I am a Strong GOD
fearing woman who loves life. I love my husband, children,
grandbabies, "Framily" (aka friends turned into family)
caring, giving, understanding, passionate about what I
believe, good listener, give advice when asked, and praying
compassionate woman.

December 30, 2016, one more day left in this year and I
woke up in Tampa, Florida with my sister Julie and Dani.
Julie has been at the hospital all night with Todd. He was
admitted a few days ago with fluid on his lungs and they
said his heart is working at 17%, I am here for them. The
purpose behind me being here and it's not just for me to get
away. GOD has a plan that we know nothing about but I

know his will is much better than ours. GOD in this moment I feel at peace with my husband being with you. He belongs to you any way you just loaned him to us for a day. 2 Peter 3:8

December 31, 2016, New Year's Eve in Tampa, Florida today has been a fun, calm, peaceful day thus far. It's 5:14 pm I will be walking into 2017 without Devan. It feels okay in this moment to say that I will be okay. My motto has become "Just Be" which is what I am doing right now. Enjoying where I am at this very moment. I remember when I would talk with my husband when he would be out of town and now I feel like I am Devan as well as myself. So tomorrow will be the start of something new and exciting. Well, maybe I shouldn't say the start because it started on September 24, 2016, when my husband transitioned from here to heaven. My spirit was being shifted and becoming something more. I was AWAKENED.

~GROWING WHILE GRIEVING~

January 3, 2017, I don't believe in New Year's Resolutions I believe that each moment is new so live in that. I am really in Tampa, Florida I actually had a nervous energy about flying here alone and look at me now I'm here and I decided to extend my stay for a few more days. I am proud of myself for stepping out on faith and living for me. Devan and I were supposed to come here this past summer but we didn't make it. So, I've promised myself not to ever put off happiness until tomorrow because we may not get tomorrow.

If we don't get tomorrow we've interrupted someone from being blessed by our existence because of our purpose in the world. The moment my husband passed I started growing to another level a higher urgent level. As I sit here I still sit in shock at the fact Devan is gone. When I picture his face, his smile, his handsomeness, and HIM! It hurts. I am being stretched beyond what I ever imagined. People say grief happens in stages. I don't think anyone can truly tell you what stage of grief you are in at any given moment.

Navigating life without him is foreign, we were like Siamese twins that have been ripped a part. Sometimes I lay in bed and I feel like I'm watching a movie and Devan and I are the leading roles. Busy is good for me, although I know I need to be still and silent at times. It's a personal journey between me and GOD. But what I do know is that I will:

- *Feel what needs to be felt in the moment*
- *Call on The Holy Spirit to comfort me in the moment*
- *I have peace knowing that my husband is in Heaven*
- *Walking by Faith and not by what it looks like*

- *Being blessed with an amazing "Squad" aka Support System*

Most importantly take care of self:

- *Spiritually*
- *Mentally*
- *Emotionally*
- *Physically*
- *Financially*

~THANKFUL, YET I CRY~

January 6, 2017, Praise and Worship this morning like every morning. Thankful, yet I cry and I can't help but wonder why. I'm not asking why because I want it to be someone else, I just miss my old life because it included him. I think I know the answer to the why... I believe because Devan did what he was called to do, also GOD has work for me to step into. I often wonder if I would've moved quicker in walking in my purpose, maybe Devan would still be here. I continue to know GOD as so many things and it's more and more intimate.

- *Healer*
- *Provider*
- *Comforter*
- *Best friend*
- *Confidant*
- *Peace*
- *Strength*
- *High Tower*
- *Protector*
- *Guide*
- *Truth*
- *Light*
- *Way*
- *Beginning*
- *Nothing Broken Nothing Missing*

~AMAZING~

On a flight, back from Tampa and it's January 7, 2017. I am looking at out the clouds and it's so amazing! I feel like I'm close to my husband it's so pretty in these clouds. When I look at my life it's very exciting and fascinating. I have truly embraced my motto: "Live in the Moment and Live out loud with no apologies." My husband lived this way and it's an amazing way to enjoy life. I asked my brother the question what if I would've walked in my purpose sooner would my husband still be with me? He said, "That has nothing to do with it." I say, that because I leaned so much on my husband .... Not in a negative insecure way but in a play, it safe type of way. I remember when Devan once told me that I had gotten comfortable I was so offended when he said those words to me but guess what it was true.

I am amazed at myself in these moments because I am not afraid anymore. I have put on my big girl undies and they fit amazingly. I am learning so much about myself and I LOVE HER!!!!!!! I am exploring and feeling things about me that I had set aside, again I'm not suggesting my husband made me not feel these things because he was/is and AMAZING MAN!!!! I think we just often times get in a rut of life and we forget to take care of us, especially women. It was GOD, Devan, my children, and then me. I didn't mind though........ but that order has changed..........
1. GOD
2. KIM
3. Everything else

My view, outlook, and perspective are so different and my lenses have changed. Let me reintroduce myself: My name is Kimberly Nicole Johnson I am an amazing GOD Fearing, Strong, Beautiful, Loving, Caring, Giving, Passionate, Compassionate, Healthy, Spiritually Grounded,

Fun, Funny, Sophisticated, Classy, Educated, Well-Traveled, Smart, Intelligent, Confident, and a Well-Rounded Woman! Nice to meet you!

January 8, 2017, woke up over Stacey and Beng's house, I stayed with them when I came back in town. That speaks volumes doesn't it I've been gone for about 11 days and I'm still not ready to go to my home. I will go home Monday morning. I have never in life been away from my home this long but things are different now.

January 9, 2017, I came back home to Cincinnati and right now in this moment I am feeling sad, lonely and, tired. I'm really missing my husband terribly. I am no longer with the man that was my best friend under Jesus. Everyone around me has someone I felt like Devan and I was the connector with everyone.

January 10, 2017, I had a rough day yesterday I came home from being away for 11 days and I thought I would be able to come and relax. I was so sad and down because being here without Devan is hard. Everything around me is him and us although no matter where I go, it's us. Being in the house, our house is difficult for me. I didn't realize that until I came back from Tampa. I just sat still yesterday and allowed myself to feel what I was feeling. I didn't get any sleep at all last night and at this very moment, I FEEL like I don't know what to do. So in these moments, I need to bring it all in..... and just BE..... in this moment!

~MOMENTS TURN INTO MEMORIES~

January 14, 2017

Today is the day we honor my husband but he isn't here, it feels like I am attending his service all over again. We are honoring a man that left a mark in this world that will never be erased. He's been gone for three months and two weeks. It's going to be amazing everyone that is a part of this event is doing it for the love of Devan and our family.

The love that so many people have shown is beyond words for me I didn't know people loved my husband and me this much. Why must we wait until someone dies to honor them? Why can't we have tributes while they're alive? It was bitter sweet watching all the performers and especially our children on stage performing their dad's songs. Our oldest son had given up performing and Devan told him the week of his passing that he would get back on stage soon. We now understand how true those words would be.

When I walked into the event and I saw each one of my children dressed like their dad would have dressed them, my heart was so full. GOD, you already knew we would be here in this moment and you already knew we would feel this pain. I expected more people to show up because of who Devan was/is but those that came were who were supposed to be there. My big sissy totally surprised me and flew in just for the event. I had no idea at all, but it meant the world to me. Stacey, Carmen, my children, "my brothers" and all were there to help make the event a success as well.

~WHAT MUST I DO TO FALL IN LOVE WITH MYSELF? ~

I must accept where I am, who I am, and where I've been.
Walk in authenticity with no apologies.
Show up honestly
Love your flaws and all
Love every part of what makes you... You feel
Love and allow yourself to be loved
Words are Powerful

January 17, 2017, I got a call today from the police investigator; this is all coming after a very emotional weekend. They said they are finished with the case and it appears to them that it was an accident. According to them, Devan just lost control of his bike. What do you mean he just lost control? This doesn't match what was told to me by the person that saw it all.

I was told by one of his bike buddies that he was at the light; he saw another guy that he would sometimes ride with, they chatted briefly then, agreed to meet up at our house to ride together. He said the light turned green then Devan's bike started to "rev" really loud. The throttle was stuck and from what I've been told he had been having some issues with the throttle, his bike launched forward and went up into a wheelie.

Well, Devan never did tricks on his bike so when that happened I'm sure he was stunned. He then stood up on the bike to put his weight on it so that would bring it back down. I was told at that point there was a parked car that was right in front of him so he swerved to avoid hitting the car. As he did that it was two girls walking down the street toward him.

One of the girls said she saw him coming and she thought he was going to hit them. She said his eyes were so big and you could tell he was really scared. She said that he saved their lives because he again swerved the bike, but when he did the last time he hit a pole which spun the bike around right into another pole. He was then ejected from the bike; he went high in the air, landed on his left side, and hit his head and my husband passed away instantly. His whole left side was hurt he had a broken arm and his left eye socket was crushed. This is hard for me to accept because my husband knew how to ride his bike with his eyes closed.

We had a Tribute for Devan it was very nice, but so heartbreaking at the same time. Antwaun performed along with other amazing artists. It was so hard watching our son perform because he said he was done with that life. The week of Devan passing someone asked Antwaun if he was still doing music and he said "No" then Devan said, "yes he still does it." Antwaun was adamant about not ever doing it again, Devan turned to him and said, "son you will do it again" not knowing those words would mean more than we thought.

Stages

I woke up today 1-21-17 extremely hurt and mad I woke at 6:30 am. I laid there wondering why I couldn't wake up with my husband next to me. I feel so alone some days like I'm a wanderer in the world alone. As much as I love my home, it's getting harder to be there without my husband. GOD blessed the US with that house and there is no US anymore. I hate feeling like a burden to my family, I hate feeling like an obligation and I know that's not their truth. The enemy will try to plant those seeds inside my mind at times. I felt like I wanted to just destroy everything in sight this morning. I had so much rage I wanted to kick and throw things, but I know that wouldn't help or change anything. I think I'm going through all of the stages of grief

67

all at once.

Denial
Anger
Depression
Bargaining
Acceptance

I have been feeling anger a lot lately and sadness!
According to the Bible, this too shall pass.

~PROCESSING~

I realized that my walk started before my husband passed away. I knew I wanted more and wanted to be great, so deciding to walk in my purpose, realizing my life would never be the same ever again. Wanting and choosing to be great. Realizing life is short so it sent a question of why, but why NOT!

January 22, 2017, sometimes I feel like just throwing in the towel. But I know GOD would be so unhappy with me. It would show that I'm not trusting him. Somedays I think I have progressed I feel like I'm going backwards.

January 25, 2017, some days I feel like I'm moving backward, it's been four months to the date, (24th) yesterday that my love has been with GOD. I wonder how long I will cry for him, yearn for him, miss him, need him, and want him? I have to stay in the present "moment" in order to move to the next "moment." I gotta keep going. I feel like a wanderer sometimes because I don't know what this is supposed to look like. None of my circle has experienced this type of loss before except me, just like I'm the only one that went through Breast Cancer.

January 31, 2017, the moment you realize that it's something missing. Things will change but will you be ready? Will you be ready for what GOD has for you? I had no choice about being ready. I feel very fragile right now, today is the last day of the month and of course, I'm missing Devan more as the days go by.

February 2, 2017, today is Devan Rmoni Johnson birthday my husband would've celebrated 44 years in this world today. First birthday without him I have no words today. Well, I do have words but it's the same words I have every day. I went to lunch with one of our close friends. I enjoyed it because he wanted to make sure I wasn't alone today. I love my family and friends, so dearly I thank GOD for them all. I don't know how someone could get through this without "the squad"

February 5, 2017, I haven't been able to write lately this is my first day writing since my husband's birthday. I cried off and on all day on Devan's birthday. I've been a little unfocused these past days I haven't been concentrating on my writing. It's hard to focus mentally. I went to a basketball game with my sisters Stacey and Carmen in Indianapolis yesterday we had fun it was just about sister time. I have moments when I feel like I'm just moving along without experiencing but then things like this happen:

I saw the most amazing rainbow as we were driving but it hadn't even rained. I thought rainbows came from the rain. Devan is that a sign from heaven that you're with me.

I had a chance to go to the salon yesterday early before anyone was there for the first time since Devan's passing. I praised and worshipped, talked to GOD, and GOD told me "I got you daughter just don't stop trusting me" Sometimes it's too much BUT GOD.

Days Turning into Months

February 7, 2016, it has been 82 days of this new life that I've been forced to experience without my husband. I say forced because it wasn't my choice. My choice would be to have my husband right here with me. I am walking into something so amazing and I must say again it's all GOD and none of me. What do you do in this moment? How do you go on? I look out to the future and I sometimes feel sad because I am now walking this alone without him.

I told my sister the other day that the best way for me to look at this journey is to see the right now. Meaning if I have 40 levels to climb; I don't focus on the 40 in front, I look at how many I've climbed so far. So, if I've climbed 3 levels already I don't look at what's ahead I look at how many I've left behind. I then look at each step in front of me; because if I look at the journey ahead, it can look very scary, and very hard but when I look back I see my progress. It goes with the saying, "How do you eat an elephant? One bite at a time.....and in the words of one of my sisters, she said, "An elephant taste nasty and we don't want to eat it all, even one bite at a time. It is hard because it doesn't taste good, but if you decide an elephant taste great, then you'll change your attitude about that one bite at a time. 'Julie Bodnar'

February 9, 2017, today is Thursday I came home Tuesday night and I slept every bit of 2 hours. Last night wasn't any better falling asleep from 10:30 pm – 2 am then back up at 5am-7am. Now it's time for me to go see my trainer I've been listening to my praise and worship all morning.

February 10, 2017, I realized in this moment that I miss the masculine energy that my husband gave me I'm so used to being handled like fine china which means very delicately. My husband was very affectionate and he always made sure that I knew how much he was attracted to me. Does this mean I will never have that again? Would my husband want me alone for the rest of my life? Of course, he wouldn't I'm nowhere near being ready to even think about being with anyone however it has crossed my mind. I miss being held, loved, caressed all of the things that come with being one with someone. I feel like a new baby learning about their world for the 1st time learning the do's and don'ts, what is, what isn't all while loving their independence as they scoot, crawl, walk then run.

~DETERMINATION~

I'm doing it, I'm really doing it, I can't believe that I AM really doing this!! My husband always said I could but wow! I am a big girl living this amazing life without the Love of my life, how is that even possible? I never imagined I would one day have to ponder that question. I am sitting inside an airplane headed to Tampa, Florida and I'm sitting next to a man that isn't my husband. I'm looking out the window at this beautiful morning wondering what my husband is doing and thinking. I feel like he's looking down saying, "Bae, I told you that you could do it" I'm picturing him talking to GOD about me.

My husband's passing is teaching me so many things about "Kim," the woman I was and showing me the woman I'm evolving into. I compare it to being an alien dropped on a new planet learning and exploring life, everything is different. There are tons of books written on how to handle grief but truth be told no one can tell you how to handle losing someone. It's a second by second walk and it's your walk. However, for me, GOD is my constant for sure and everything else falls under him. I'm walking without my cane which was my husband, there are moments I feel unfocused, unmotivated and just lost with the thoughts of life but I bring it all back to "moment by moment"

February 19, 2017, Forty-three was the age that things shifted for both Devan and me, four plus three is seven. GOD completed everything in seven days. Was it because it was the beginning of my life and my walk into my purpose but the end of his purpose which he fulfilled. What does this mean? My husband passed away at the young age of 43 which is the same year I was diagnosed with Breast Cancer. I/we beat that and almost three years later he is gone. Talk about processing wow!

As I sit here and write these words it's mind boggling to think about it. I often try to figure out the purpose of it all. GOD allowed us to walk through that journey together but yet I'm walking this one without him. My husband used to always ask me "What would you do if I wasn't here" why would he ask me that? What was I being prepared for? He was preparing me for the now, for this purpose, my purpose and he was doing it unknowingly. I never imagined my life without my soulmate. So, whenever he asked me that I would simply say "Well, I don't have to ever worry about that." Yet, I am walking in that very statement.

The answer has now changed, I am trusting the process, walking step by step, moment by moment, authentically and I am not alone. I know GOD is with me and I can feel my husband with me. I think about him in every movement and thought he is my driving force to keep going. He is the reason I haven't given up I feel like he has passed the baton to me and it's my turn to run the race. I can do it, as a matter of fact, I want to do it. So many people think I can't do it without him but it's not about what they think it's about what has been placed inside of me.

I have so much clarity it all makes sense it is so crystal clear. Did my husband have to pass for me to walk in my purpose? Was he done walking in his? I know that I've been catapulted into mine. I guess I wasn't moving fast enough I will never delay my life ever again, I will never be second to anyone or anything. Did I love my husband more than GOD unknowingly? There are people waiting for me to share my purpose it's not just for me. Like I've said how can I go through all this and be the same? It's impossible and frankly, I don't want to be the same. I get it! I got it! It so clear! My heart belongs to me now so what does that mean? So many questions? I have days that I feel like I'm in a trance like I'm just going through the motions, existing

73

but not fully present.

February 20, 2017, I am tanning in February this time last year I was preparing to have surgery. My life is what Devan and I use to talk about. He would say, "Bae, think about where you want to live." I always said Miami and I'm in Tampa right this moment. I never imagined that I would be here living the dreams we shared together but doing it without him. When I think too far out it creates panic and anxiety so I have to pull myself back into the moment. I feel like I'm living my life for the both of us. I know my husband is smiling on me.

~PROCESSING and CLARITY~

Will I feel any of these things ever again? Does GOD not want me to experience that type of love of course he does. He is love when you've been in love with someone for 20 plus years you aren't only just grieving the loss of them. You're going to grieve "everything" that comes along with them no longer being in the world. I have had my husband's' love every single day for over 20 plus years. I miss his touch, his kisses, his hugs, his prayers, his laugh, his smile, his passion, his LOVE!

These are the things most people take for granted, am I supposed to not be? GOD is love so how can that be his plan? I am learning what I want in all of this, I am reinventing who I am, I'm experiencing a rebirth an awakening of some sort. It's very scary yet exciting and it's very important that you don't stop loving yourself in this process. Put on makeup, go get a haircut, get your hair done, put on some nice clothes, buy yourself something amazing self-love and care play a big role in the "processing" of it all.

It's been five months and I'm still processing and I'm not afraid to admit that I'm scared at times. I have so many decisions that I must make and I'm making them without my husband. That's a very scary place to be because Devan and I are one. I realize that it's me here and I can't allow fear to arrest my mind, body, and soul. I must continue to move forward at this stage and I am not afraid to ask for help. Every stage requires support from "the squad" because they're a very big part of this grieving process.

In this stage, it's also important to begin to not just process but begin to accept what is. The acceptance will come in waves I'm learning that no one can tell you how to grieve or feel. I do know that it's very important to feel what you need to feel in those moments it doesn't matter when or where. Just release and process.

February 22, 2017, I'm on the plane waiting to go back to Cincinnati, we are delayed but I've realized that delays are for a purpose. I know that Gods hands are on us and that he's protecting us from something. While in Tampa I went to see a Nirvana Spiritualist Doctor I was skeptical at first because I operate under The Blood of Jesus and the Holy Spirit. I wanted to make sure she did as well. As soon as I walked in I felt The Holy Spirit present so I instantly relaxed. We had an instant connection she already knew a lot about me. Dr. Sandi isn't a regular acupuncture doctor she can feel your energy. She told me that I'm scared. I said, "scared of what being here with you now'? She said no you're scared of your new life, that I'm now walking in. As she was putting the pins in my body & she got to the side of the body that holds grief she became very emotional. She said to me "your grief is very heavy & somedays you are so depressed & blue I began to cry because she was right. It felt good to know that someone felt my pain. She also knew about the issues with "my father" She told me I needed to forgive him and release him so I could begin to move forward with that as well. When I left that day, I felt so relaxed like I just had a bottle of wine. This is something new in my life that is helping me with this grief.

February 24, 2017, my sister called me today and told me what Dr. Sandi told her today about me she said "I love all of your friends but your sister she's very special I love Kim a little more. My sister asked her why was I a little special to her? She said Kim is marked by GOD. She is strong and that I must finish the book. I'm very special like she is as well as my sister. I receive all of that because I know it's The Holy Spirit speaking to me through her.

Just Be

People ask me what it means to Just Be" and the answer to that question is simple. It means to be whatever you're feeling at that very moment and embrace whatever that is. If it's negativity then choose to change it and that means you have to be present with how you're feeling. We tend to focus on what next I'm guilty of doing the same thing at times. I mentioned earlier how Devan would ask me "Bae, what would you do if I wasn't here"? He would ask me that if I would call him for something that I could figure out for myself and I would think of something smart to say but I would say, "We don't have to worry about that do we" and I wondered today when I woke up if my answer was wrong. My answer should've been I will always have GOD. Did I lean more on my husband than GOD? I've always put GOD first or so I thought..... Well now I have no other choice it's the best choice.

I finally had my husband's cell phone removed from my account which meant they had to cut the service off. Does that mean he's being erased? I called his number and it's not his number anymore. How do I feel about that? In this moment I'm feeling numb but isn't this a part of moving forward while grieving? I have taken up acupuncture and I've realized that I've been stuck, I don't want to stay stuck being stuck gives birth to stagnation I want and need to continue to grow while grieving. Which means actively handling our business now "my business" although it's very painful because it's shutting doors and forcing me to look ahead without Devan. Am I ready to move ahead without him is the question, and the answer is that I have no choice. Think about what it means to grow, to change physically, to come to know something over time.

I was having a pain in my right leg and I realized it was

because of my resistance to growing and moving forward because I thought I was leaving Devan behind I don't want to be resistance. I have realized that our house was made for our family so when I come home I can feel something is missing. So I subconsciously stay away and when I look around our house I see what Devan and I built, which was a home full of love, laughter and GOD yet my husband is missing. I can't keep running from it I must face it, walk in it so I can get through it. In these moments, we need support from our family and friends.

I'm so glad I enjoyed Devan that gives me peace knowing that we were best friends. He would always say "we are all we have" I would say we have our children and he said, "I know Bae, but you and I are all we really have," He's no longer here so what do I have? Yet, I know that I'm loved so much more by GOD, I truly know that its purpose in all of this grief and it isn't to make me sad, go ball up in the corner and give up.

I am discovering who Kimberly Nicole Johnson is in all of this. I already know who Mrs. LaDevan Johnson is but who is Kimberly? I like who I'm discovering, I like who I'm meeting because she isn't afraid, she's spontaneous, she's authentic, she's caring, she's open to what GOD has in store because it's good. I had to walk through all those storms to birth "her" so again moment by moment. It's about releasing negative energy and operating off our positive vibrations simply choosing to 'Just Be" We often say or ask, "why me" well why not you? Why not?

February 28, 2017, today is the last day of the month and this time last year I was having surgery to remove my right breast and begin reconstruction after beating Breast Cancer. Actually, I had surgery Feb 29, 2016, which is very symbolic to a certain degree because we only have that date every four years I don't have to celebrate that date because from the beginning of that journey it was done that date just sealed it forever.

So today I sit here reflecting back on that day excited about the closure that was taking place in that moment. I must admit that was not a fun surgery it was also a very painful recovery because of all the drains I had to have. At the same time, it was doing something inside of me and I had my husband with me so it was easy to go through. Wow, how amazing is GOD he knew I would be sitting here in this moment wondering why. While knowing that he will get the glory from it all.

March 4, 2017, waking up listening to my praise and worship *I'll trust you GOD! * The space I'm in right now is the way I felt the day my husband left this world. I begged and pleaded with GOD not to take my husband. But it was time for Devan to go. I've had a few people say to me that GOD didn't take Devan that he had nothing to do with what happened. That's saying that GOD isn't in control of everything or that he can be caught if guard and that's not true.

March 7th, 2017, flying again what does that mean? Who has emerged because of this pain? I have been awakened and I am feeling peace in this moment. I have chosen to live instead of giving up rolling over and dying. I feel my husband's spirit within me. I am so much like him or am I so much like me? My goal in life is to LIVE OUT LOUD.... NO regrets. I am literally above the clouds right now and it's amazing losing my husband has catapulted me into this 'NEW' place in life.

When was the last time you can say that you were truly happy? It isn't a trick question it's a real question. My husband is gone never to return and yet I'm walking in peace and happiness. I am excited about my journey that's before me and frankly, I don't think that I would've ever walked this path if my husband was still here. He told me a week before his transition that I was too comfortable and I was so offended by those words and you know why? Because it was true!

I had gotten so comfortable with my life being so mundane, with going to the salon every day, not even doing hair just being there because I just wanted to be around my husband. After going through breast cancer I realized doing hair was no longer my passion and I didn't know how to tell my husband I lost it. Which was why I started having the feeling like something was missing inside of me. I was already walking in my transition and didn't even realize that my road had already started to change.

If someone would've told me this was going to be my life a year ago I would've "NEVER" believed them, because I knew that I was going to be married to the same man until we grew old and gray. Plus how and why would GOD allow such a thing? Well, here I stand! I have discovered a strength I never ever knew existed. I guess it speaks to the saying "You never know how strong you are until you "have" to know how strong you are. I have wondered if my husband was caught in the cross fire of me being thrust into this new life I'm in. What I mean is this, did I not move fast enough for my purpose? Was I supposed to move after the breast cancer journey? Did I hear and not listen? Was my story of surviving supposed to start there? I will forever have this question inside of me and I'm sure I will never get the answer that will suffice for me. So what do I do now I can't stay angry right or can I? Did I do this? Is this my fault?

As I sit here writing in Tampa I am shedding tears thinking about that man who was my everything! If I look back or to the side I will fall so I continue to look ahead. I can hear my family laughing in the kitchen and I love it even though I'm missing my husband because I have peace with what my life is unfolding into.

When I talk to people and they share their trials in life I tell them to choose to be happy and I'm sure they may think "how can she tell me that? She has no idea." Well, I believe I have some wisdom in that area. The year 2014 is when my transition started to take place, Jan we found out that everyone in our salon was leaving all at once. That was a blow because it was all done very deceitfully we had no idea. That same month was one of the coldest winters we had in a while and our furnace went out along with our pipes bursting.

In February, we got a call from one of our sons from the county jail saying he was in some trouble which was slightly devastating and it took almost a year to deal with that situation. Two months later in April, I was diagnosed with Breast Cancer. Okay GOD, what's going on did I do something to you are you mad at me? The next 18 months were a journey and we conquered that journey together! Yes, I said together because that's what you do when you're one in the same. We did it we enjoyed each moment of life even in that we didn't ball up and waste time sulking in any of it. All the while we are being molded, formed, shaped into these people that the world would soon know in a way that we could only imagine.

Two years and five months later my husband is gone, not because we separated, divorced, but because he was done in this world. Wait, what do you mean he's gone? Gone where my husband would never leave me alone. He was my guardian angel he always protected me and took good care of me so why would he leave? Okay, so we went through all of that to then turn around and lose my husband? So when someone says to me I don't understand well I think I have qualifications to say I highly understand. I am choosing to be happy while grieving yet growing. I could choose to take drugs, ball up in a corner but I must keep going.

March 8, 2017, I have to pinch myself at times because I have to make sure I'm really experiencing this. I'm in awe of how GOD is working in my life. I'm so grateful, thankful, and blessed. I say Thank you to GOD a million times a day. I had an off day yesterday, I couldn't figure out what it was so this morning I realized what happened. Every day since my husband has been gone I wake up pray, talk to GOD and listen to praise and worship before I step out of the bed. However yesterday my routine was thrown off I did listen to some praise and worship, I did pray, but because I was preparing to come back to Tampa my routine was shifted.

As I went to the airport, my spirit was different but brushed it off because I was in route. The feeling became more intense then my mind tried to start playing tricks with negative thoughts like *you're by yourself- where is your husband? -What would happen if something happened to you right now? My heart started beating fast like I was having an anxiety attack. I called my sister and she talked me through it. I was nervous because the last time I felt like that was after I had first surgery to remove left breast and

Devan left to go pick up the meds the doctor prescribed to me. I instantly became nervous and I thought I was about to have a panic attack and my sister had to talk me through that until Devan came back. That's what that moment felt like which means I will never disrupt my routine again it's vital, it's a part of my "growing while grieving"

March 10, 2017, I just arrived to Ana Maria Island and it's

*absolutely beautiful yet, I am so sad again in this moment.
How long will I cry, ache, hurt, and miss my husband?
How long will I feel this pain that's sometimes unbearable?
Why do I have to feel it? So many questions with no
answers, at least not any which would satisfy me. I am
sitting in this big amazing house currently in tears. I cry
every day for the loss of my husband but these past few
days I've cried more, am I just now settling into my reality?*

*My husband should be on this island with me. I shouldn't
have to do this without him yet I am. And frankly, I'm
highly upset about it. What does GOD expect from me?
GOD, you really want me to live this life without him?
When I ask these questions I simply hear GOD saying 'Yes
I do' I know what's best for you so just continue to trust me
daughter.*

*March 14, 2017, everyone grieves but not everyone mourns
which means to express openly and release it's a part of
healing.*

PEACE

*In this moment I feel peace around me I can feel my
husband. I think about my children and their families and I
feel like I'm not there for them like I use to be. They're so
very amazing because they are allowing me to "Just Be"
they're very supportive I don't want to look up one day and
my grandchildren are all grown. But I am walking my
purpose not just for me but also for them and their future.*

*I have a legacy just like my husband and I am walking in it.
His place of peace comes and goes I'm learning how to
embrace these moments because they are vital for the
process of healing. I've heard that peace is a state of mind
which I agree with partially but peace to me is being*

completely still while listening and hearing GOD and being fully present in the moment receiving it. Peace to me is also a state of being and choosing to be. No-one can give you peace except GOD. Let go of all the negative energy and flow in positive energy.

March 17, 2017, heading to Miami with my big sissy Julie and baby sis Stacey. I am doing this without Devan the last time I was in Miami I was with him. I'm letting go of all the negative energy and I'm embracing all the positive energy GOD has for me. I'm choosing to do that, I choose to embrace this moment we will never it again. We will never have the same experience twice.

March 20, 2017, yesterday was an emotional day for me I hadn't cried the two days prior which felt weird to some degree. I just got back from an awesome vacation with two of my sisters and I was feeling good. The trip to Miami was bittersweet as most of my life has been these past six months. I have learned when those moments of pain come to disrupt my peace to stop, recognize and acknowledge the feeling, allow myself to feel what I need to in those moments. Connect with the creator by walking, standing barefoot with the earth receiving every good intention that's for me and releasing sad, bad intentions from me. Take three deep inhales and exhales again release and receive. Water also resets the chakras so we can be authentic I am so at peace in this very space and moment.

My daughters came to visit me in Tampa which is adding to my peace. Peace isn't something anyone can give you except the Holy Spirit. It's a place you have to be willing to be open to. I don't want to live in turmoil even though my life has been shifted around totally. I asked GOD yesterday why this is my life. Why is my husband gone so soon? Some days it gets very hard to imagine what's next for me and my family. I look at my children and get angry sometimes because they still need their dad. I can name quite a few other people who I feel are wasting this precious gift we have each day we awake that could've left. However, I have peace knowing that GOD doesn't need any help with being GOD so that in its self is enough for me.

March 27, 2017, it has been six months since my husband has been gone, I sometimes feel it on the date of his passing. I felt it on Friday which was 3-24-17. The pain sometimes just comes out of nowhere someone asked me what triggers it. My response was, "I could see a piece of lint fall to the ground and that could trigger the pain. It can be anything there's no one thing that I can say, do or avoid that would cause or prevent the grief from seeping in. It is truly a moment by moment process no-one can give you a guide on how to deal with it. The only thing I can say is to allow yourself to feel whatever it is you're feeling in the moment so you can walk through it.

I went to see my holistic acupuncturist today she felt all of my grief energy and she said she was going to relieve me. She also said she felt my energy of me being angry. I looked at her with a question in my eyes and she said, "You have some anger towards GOD," I said, I'm not mad at GOD she said you are and it's ok to feel that, GOD is still GOD and he understands your pain. So she released a lot of that from me, she also told me that I am an author and I have purpose to not get sidetracked focus on the book. I have things to share and tell because someone needs me. I feel so much better in this moment I am not going get sidetracked how can I?

March 28, 2017, yesterday I was very emotional I slept okay but not great. Today the emotional pull in me is lingering. I hate this feeling because it feels like I'm again wandering again. So many things I feel uncertain in this moment. I stare out the window as I sit in this nail salon but I see nothing I just feel heartbroken. The calls are slow today so I feel abandoned in this very moment. Yet, I must allow myself to feel these emotions so I can move ahead in this grief process.

April 6, 2017, I have been back home for seven days today and I have cried every day since being back. The weather has been gloomy and cold. I've had to handle some major business pertaining to the house and property I own and it's been quite overwhelming. I'm used to it being "us" and not "I" I've been dealing with some major anger and hurt as well. The questions are back and I keep getting the same answer back which is "Be still and know that I am GOD"

April 7, 2017, today is important to me for two major reasons, it's the day GOD blessed us with our oldest son 30 years ago. It's also the day three years ago I was told I had Breast Cancer. (I am completely healed) Imagine hearing those words on your sons 27th birthday. Devan and I couldn't believe our ears it had to be a mistake. But GOD had a different plan he is bigger than any and everything. Devan and I knew that I was healed in that same moment. We knew the finished works of Jesus already took care of it.

I am a SURVIVOR of Breast Cancer and Losing "My DEVAN" Our life was renewed on so many levels and now he isn't physically here to walk the rest of it with me but GOD is right by my side. Thank you GOD for our son and Thank you GOD for blessing me with an amazing man who loved me/us with every fiber in his body and I love with every fiber in my body. I won't stop what you allowed Devan and I to start, I am so focused on my purpose I have overcome a lot I give all my credit to GOD because what you see is him. I just trust him through it all. My son doesn't want to celebrate his birthday because he and his dad had big plans for his 30th and now he says it isn't the same without his dad. I agree no holiday or special occasion will ever be the same. But I know that "My DEVAN" wants us to enjoy our lives, we will see him again one day so in the meantime, we will continue to live out loud!! HAPPY BIRTHDAY MY BABY

"The best teacher is the one who experiences the lesson first." "Kimberly Johnson"

~THE NOISE~

How do you quiet the noise inside of you and around you when it's all that you hear? Why is the noise so loud anyway? The noise reminds you that your situation is real, but does it mean it's your reality? It feels like you have a billion thoughts and questions all at once with no answer in sight. Like the why's, the how's, the when's, and the where's. It's been 146 days, 4 months, 3 weeks since My Devan has been in Heaven. It gets harder as the days go by. I have finally realized that it's not a dream, he is gone for good, never to return back to this place. I have thoughts of "now what?" How do I continue on without him? How do I walk without Devan? Who will protect me, laugh with me, inspire me, cry with me, and pray with and for me? Who will hold me, LOVE ME?

This is all a part of the noise, the noise that tries to take over you. So again how does one quiet the noise? I quiet the noise by listening, which means I have to be still and quiet right in the midst of the noise. You can't ignore the noise and you can't avoid the noise you must walk through all the waves of this thing called loss and grief. It's a very scary walk however if you choose not to move through you will be stuck and the noise will be forever present. The noise can make you afraid to continue, it tells you to give up, to stay right where you are.

I have chosen to move beyond the noise I will never give up. The noise is making me brave because I can hear my husband saying to me "You can do it, Bae, don't be afraid" I don't know how long the noise will last because some days there is none. Yet, some days it's so loud and I feel as though I can't even think. I must be very careful not to fall prey to the noise because if I do my purpose through all of this will be lost so I have started: Realizing and accepting the truth at this very moment which is:

- *I can make it on my own*
- *I am choosing to put one foot in front of the other*
- *Decide to allow life to flow freely without worrying about what's next*
- *Yes, it's very scary to even think about doing these things without you Devan because we were one for many decades.*

So now what? Does one stay stuck? It's a second by second walk each step is new, unfamiliar and uncertain it takes faith, courage, and trust. It feels like you are walking with a blindfold over your eyes but you know that your steps are already placed in front of you so you just walk. Also understanding that I must be patient with myself because I've just experienced one of life's most painful events at such a young age.

April 10, 2017, I cry every day, I mean every day. Sometimes alone and sometimes with others but the tears fall! Is that good? Is it bad? What does it mean? But then I realize I laugh every day sometimes alone and with others. Does that mean I'm feeling? What does it mean GOD? I cry for Devan, I cry for myself, I cry for my children, I cry for my grandchildren, I just cry! How long will this be? How many seconds, minutes, days, weeks, months, and years will I cry? Do I have enough tears? Will they run out? This is real life. I look in the mirror at myself and I just stare at the woman looking back. I'm amazed at her beauty, strength, endurance, determination, love, her SOUL! She doesn't look like what her journey has been she looks like where her journey is taking her. So amazing

"GOD will stretch us but if we go against the stretch it will hurt. We have to enjoy the stretch if we go with his stretch it's easy." "Kimberly Johnson"

~HURT~

*April 11, 2017, I can't, I can't, I can't, and I just can't!
Someone tell me how please. I'm listening to some old
school music and it hurts because it songs my husband
played and loved. I need to move out this house it's too
painful and the longer I stay the more the pain sets in.
When I walk in this house and I'm alone sometimes it just
paralyzes me. I've been asked "how are you still there in
the house" because we built the second half of our lives in
this house with our family. I've already lost him now I'm
leaving us behind or so it seems.*

*I need to move so I can close this door and continue to
heal. What am I doing? Some days I don't really know, and
I found out today that we're having another grandbaby.
This hurts me even more because Devan will not get to
meet him/her. Is it selfish of me to feel sad about that? I'm
grateful for the new life that God has decided to allow us to
have but it just feels different. Whenever we got news of
having another grandbaby we heard it together now it's
just me. I want to throw my computer, kick something over
in this moment I'm ANGRY!!!!*

*God, you have allowed this to be and it can't be changed
ever. It's been very hard to be around my grand babies
without Paw Paw with me. I miss them and I hate that I feel
this way I don't want them to ever forget him or me. We use
to see them a couple of times a week and now it's been a lot
of videos. Am I running from my life? What am I doing?
What am I doing? I went to the salon today and stayed for
about four hours which is pretty long for me since Devan
has been gone.*

*We have two new barbers that GOD sent to us and it feels
good. People often ask me if I'm going to keep the Salon*

and I say a strong YES! GOD created Incredible Creations Beauty and Barber Salon and birthed it in us. This is our child I would never give it up Devan and I worked so hard for this brand. My husband left the salon one hour on the day of his passing that was the last place I saw my husband as he walked up that hallway. Everything reminds me of my husband EVERYTHING! I thought I would make it without crying today but of course, that didn't happen. I guess allowing the tears to flow is cleansing and I know God knows how many tears I will shed the rest of my life. When I ask GOD, how can I live and go on without Devan he simply says, "You have me and I'm better than him."

April 14, 2017, I had a very weird dream last night I dreamt that I was with my shop family and I don't remember where we were but one of the barbers was telling a story and I laughed as I did that I felt my bracket on my braces pop off then all of my teeth began to fall out. I got up and went into another room so no one would see me. At that point, all of them came out plus more. I started to cry and looking at them, I noticed they were all healthy which was even more shocking to me I then woke up. I was feeling something lingering around me what is it?

Now I know what it was... I just had another breakdown I was looking through some of Devan's things and I came across a Cd case I opened it up to find all of my husband's music that he's recorded over the years and I lost it. Why did he ride his bike that day? Why didn't GOD allow his bike to not start? Where was he going? I was told that he was trying to avoid hitting two girls that got in his way as he tried to control his bike. Why didn't he just hit them was my initial thought I doubt they would've been seriously hurt. I have these moments of pure anger! But after I go through those emotions The Holy Spirit comforts me.

April 15, 2017, today marks the 1st day that I went to the

salon at 8 am since Devan has been gone. I worked at his station I felt him with me. The salon will never feel like it did when Devan was there. However; I know GOD is sending the right team to be with me to rebuild and continue what GOD allowed Devan and I to start. The passion for hair is no longer a part of me because I did this with my husband we were a team.

Our day to day togetherness was something unexplainable our flow was flawless. People use to ask us "how is it working with your spouse every day"? Our answer was simple. We love each other, we like each other, we make each laugh, we have fun and we're best friends! Not many people are blessed to have these dynamics in their marriage. I enjoy the customers and I love having our salon but I don't feel that thing you are supposed to feel when you're operating in your purpose and passion which tells me that I have surpassed being a hairstylist maybe it will come back but for now it's gone. And if I'm completely honest with myself it left before my husband left this world. That's why I had that conversation with him the Tuesday before he transitioned about something being missing. I know without any doubts that I am now walking in my ultimate purpose.

April 16, 2017, today is Resurrection Sunday the day Jesus got up Thank you GOD for this precious gift. I'm in our house having praise and worship thinking about My Devan" thinking about what we did last year and what we would be doing right now today. I asked GOD why couldn't he be here and GOD keeps telling me "I'm here" Another "holiday" without him. Devan gets to spend this day with Jesus how amazing is that. My husband probably hasn't stopped talking yet.

Letter to My Devan

Dear Husband,

Today is Resurrection Day I'm missing you more than my words can ever say. I would say more than you know but that's not true because you know how much I miss you. You are sitting with Jesus watching over us and I can feel you with me. I know that you're so proud of me and you don't want me sad. I'm really trying hard not be sad but it's hard because you were my world. You would always say "Bae, we are all we have" and now I don't have you.

Sometimes I get upset with you because I feel like you just left me here to figure things out on my own. But I know it was time for you to go, you had no choice and I know that it wasn't up to you. I have embraced so many things that you use to do but I guess because we are /were, one that's going to happen. Your children miss you they have some tough days but I know you're with them. Ryan and Drea are having another baby we will have nine grandbabies.

I must admit I was sad when I first heard the news because you will not be here to see the baby born. We did everything together husband everything GOD created us and I know he needs no help being who he is. I miss you every second of the day, I think about you even more than that. I have been spending a lot of time with Big Sis and Big Brother in Tampa and guess what I think I am going to actually move there. They love me so much and you already know how I feel about them GOD answered every prayer regarding me having a big sister she is the big sister I use to tell you I wish I always had funny how she was always in my life the entire time.

I wish you would've had a chance to come to Tampa with me. You were so overjoyed when I told you that I found her and was excited about us going there to visit but we never made it physically together. I am surrounded by so much love husband and I feel you with me. I cry for you not from depression but because I just miss everything about the man GOD gave me 20 years ago. I will continue to be who GOD created me be I never thought I would be able to take another step in this world without you in it... but GOD!

I LOVE YOU HUSBAND FOREVER

April 18, 2017, I have to pinch myself sometimes because I often can't believe that this is my reality. I had a phone conversation today with the president/CEO of The African American Chamber and they would like to honor my husband Devan and induct him into The Black Business Hall of Fame May 20, 2017. To say that I'm in awe is understating my emotions, my husband has left a mark that can never be erased. GOD has a purpose for everything he allows. I think if my husband wasn't walking in his purpose and was in the world creating havoc things would be different. GOD allowed my husband to leave this world when he did because he is GOD.

However, I'm understanding the purpose I have in the world due to my husband leaving this place if that makes sense. So I will accept the award on behalf of the most amazing man I know. God is elevating me in ways I haven't even begun to see. I wish Devan would've received some of these accolades will he was alive. We must start honoring people in this world so they can physically enjoy the fruits of their labor.

I went to see an apt/condo today and I again can't believe I have to do this. I have never lived alone and frankly, it's quite scary and exciting at the same time. The people ask me questions like "What's your budget?" How many bedrooms do you need? When do you need to move? I *wanted to yell "I DON'T KNOW'!!!!!!!! How am I supposed to have the answers to these questions? Why must I have the answers to these questions?*

April 23, 2017, waking up in Tampa, Florida and it's amazing I have a different feeling when I wake up here. My energy is different, my vibrations are different as well. I feel peaceful and calm I haven't cried since last Thursday is that good or bad? What does that mean?

April 24, 2017, today marks seven months since my husband's passing the days and months just keep passing me by. I spoke too soon yesterday about not crying because I unleashed tears this morning. My tears are for me, our children and family we think about Devan every day, every second. I woke up today choosing to be happy although the enemy was trying me. First with one of our sons he called to try to talk about him and his girlfriend, but I shut that down because they have to learn how to lean into GOD.

Just like my husband use to say "what would you do if I wasn't here?" Now, I'm not in that space to get involved and I will always be a mom; however, they are all grown. It's time for me to do me and start living this new life. GOD has it all under control and he needs no help from us. Actually, I'm kind of shocked at myself yet impressed because I use to drop everything for my kids when they went through stuff it was times when Devan would get frustrated with me because I was too involved with them. He wanted them to handle things themselves. My husband never went to his mom about nothing, he went to GOD about everything which is who we all should go to. He was really teaching me and preparing me for this moment.

April 26, 2017, yesterday was melancholy although it was a very pretty day I felt the spirit of sadness following me I instantly prayed for GOD to rebuke that away from me considering my circumstances, But when I walked back in my sister's house and into my room I felt alone, lonely I felt as though that spirit was trying to hang around like how a pesky fly won't go away until you finally kill it. I reached out to one of my sisters she walked me through that space. My phone was pretty quiet yesterday which made me feel like no one was thinking about me. My baby boy called me and we talked earlier in the day and I had a few other calls. But I didn't get the call that I long for, the call I will forever miss, the call that would make my day. It is so painful just knowing my husband is never going to call me again. Some days I feel like, "Okay Kim you can do this and then other moments when I ask myself, "What are you doing?"

I slept really good I opened my eyes at 8 am after going to sleep around midnight. I did my usual routine which is before I step one foot out the bed I talk to God, I pray then go into Praise and Worship, talked with my sisters, had my morning tea then got ready so I could go to the gym and workout. It's so pretty outside the sun feeds my soul I'm making connections in Tampa. Devan has an old client that now lives here which was pretty cool to know and he owns a gym. How small is the world that I would run into someone I knew? Again this goes back to my husband and who he was to the world.

I feel so focused right in this moment. I also woke up with a purpose to be amazingly great today. Today is all we have at this moment not tomorrow but right now, not yesterday but now. We all have a puzzle to complete and that puzzle is called life each day represents a new piece to the puzzle that will one day be complete. If you've ever worked on a puzzle each piece has a great significance to the next piece. If the piece doesn't fit the puzzle will not make sense or be complete.

April 30, 2017, today is the last day of April I woke up at 7:28 am I thought I would've slept longer. I had my children on my mind upon waking because one of our sons and his girlfriend are having issues. Issues that are normal in relationships especially for a couple in their 20's. Me being a mom would be in their mix trying to make sure that they settled their disagreements but not anymore. My husband would always tell me to stay out of it. He would say they have to learn how to handle their own relationships. I would get upset with him and he didn't care about me being mad. He simply would say that they are men and they can't run to mom and dad all the time. I just wanted to fix it for them but now I understand and what's even more amazing for me is that I don't feel bad not one bit. I don't have what they need from me at this point and time of my life. It has to be about Kim and my purpose because it's been about them and my husband for 30 years.

May 1, 2017, I slept until 8:30 am which is a good sleep for me because I have been waking up at 2, 3, and 4 am. I thought I would forever wake up at those hours for the rest of my life but GOD said no, I will give you sweet sleep. This morning however I could feel it was going to be an emotional day for me. Sometimes I can feel when it's going to hit and other times it just hit's you like a ton of bricks.

Mondays sometimes ignite the grief, not to mention it's the first day of the month which further solidifies the fact that he isn't coming back. Each day pushes him further behind me. It's like when you're driving away from someone and the further you go the smaller they become in the rearview mirror until you can no longer see them that's what it feels like to me as the days and months go by.

Since my husband is being inducted into The Black Business Hall of Fame I needed to have some alterations done to my gown which again is emotional for me. I think today will be one of those days that I'm emotional all day I embrace these feelings so that I can walk through them. I was talking to someone today and during the talk had another emotional breakdown. I was told that I need to find a way to get a grip or grasp on my emotions and to use some type of self-control with my emotions because they don't want to see me still in a place of sadness for the next year three to five years.

My response was simple, "If it was that easy to get a grip or grasp of my emotions, I would never cry, I would feel, nothing." This man wasn't just any man to me he was my partner in life for over 20 years. No one can tell me how long I should or shouldn't grieve for my husband. I also understand that everyone will not be able to walk this walk with me and that's okay. I don't want anyone to tolerate me I want people to want to want to walk with me.

GOD knows who is for the trip and who isn't I am so blessed to have the people in my life that I have. I had a talk with my sister today and we are planning my birthday party. I wasn't going to do anything special for my birthday because I felt like it would to be the same without Devan. It will be different, however, I truly know this is what he would want me to do. I haven't celebrated a birthday without my husband so once again another bittersweet moment. Our son has a birthday in nine days and he's never had one without his dad. He will be 24 years old and Devan will not see it.

May 3, 2017, Heading back to Cincinnati from Tampa I have some engagements that I need to handle and I'm going to look at some apartments when I land. I have another photo shoot, Devan's tribute event, I'm speaking at the Relay for Life event all in the month of May. I am learning something amazing about myself each and every day. I saw Dr. Sandi my holistic acupuncture doctor yesterday she released a lot of the energy inside of me relating to emotions due to the grief.

Monday and Tuesday were a little rough for me but I made it through because I called on The Holy Spirit and he comes right away. I had another dream with Devan in it but he isn't talking to me like most of my dreams. I dreamed about him every night; I usually can't remember them but I know they are about him. He was sitting at a table with two of his brothers, then I walked in. One of his brothers got up and started walking with me. As we walked away I looked back at Devan he was watching me as I walked away with his brother almost like he was saying, "I'm right here it's okay" I see you and I'm not going anywhere. I am starting to see signs that he is with me.

I had a conversation with one of my sons the other day and we were talking about moving forward without Dad. I began to tell him how each day is purposeful and intentional for me and that I make an effort to be in the moment. I told him that I never would've imagined this to be my life even in my wildest dreams or nightmares. He said mom, as a young child I've watched you and you are so strong. He went on to say how he's always knows that about me. I never knew that my children felt that way about me. I know that they love the ground both Devan and I walk on but I didn't realize that they were paying that much attention to me.

May 4, 2017, the first Thursday of May is today and what a day it is. I woke up praising GOD being grateful as I am talking to my sister about GOD and my son comes over and tells me that they are towing my car. I freaked out right in the midst of praising GOD. They said that I had $780.00 worth of tickets. Now I'm upset because I took care of those tickets. So why is this happening I was just speaking about how good GOD was? I allowed my emotions to take control in that moment. I went to handle the business of taking care of all the things that concerned the car. I choose to have a good day despite my morning because at the end of it all GOD wants me to know that he is with me period.

Now I'm home and I walk in the house and I hear water leaking and guess what it is? The water heater on the third floor which is where our bedroom suite is. This is something my husband would typically take care of but he isn't here so it goes back to the question he would often ask me "what would you do if I wasn't here" I have learned the answer to that question because I am living the answer. I would turn to GOD and I have turned and leaned into GOD for everything. While giving thanks in all things no matter what. The verdict is I need to get a new water heater for the top floor but why should I get another one when I will be moving soon. As the plumber was talking I was just thinking about how GOD blessed us with this house it wasn't meant for just one of us. I think I may need to get some rest this day has been long but I know it's just another day that has a purpose and is another piece to the puzzle.

May 5, 2017, Waking up to heavy rain this morning I don't feel like getting up just yet although I'm grateful for this day. I have an appointment with the videographer for the African American Chamber so I can be interviewed for the gala. The interview was very emotional because I'm talking about my husband and use and one of our sons stayed here last night because of their dynamics at home and frankly I want no parts of it. I told my kids that the mom they're use to is no longer in existence, she vanished when their father left this world. This rain is so depressing to my soul I absolutely hate the rain yet I know it's very important because it makes things grow while cleansing but I have to go home and face the truth.

I had the plumber turn the hot water off on the hot water heater upstairs because basically, it's no good which means that I can only use the cold water in my bathroom. However, Devan's shower in his bathroom works fine. Now, I haven't been in his bathroom since he passed away, that was his sanctuary a place that he would be in for hours creating music, writing, talking to GOD just being Devan. I only took a shower in his bathroom twice before this moment and now GOD is making me face this now. This is another hard moment for me it's so many dynamics to losing my husband, so many things that I must face. I think that I have been procrastinating with a lot of things but it's time to face it.

As I walk in the house I hang around downstairs again prolonging what I must do. As I walk up the stairs to take off my clothes I walk past his man cave I stare into his room with all of his clothes again realizing that I will need to tackle that very soon as well. Ok, so now it's time to go inside his bathroom so that I can clean it up and start going through his things. As I stand inside I looked up at one of his mirrors and I remember the message I wrote on it in lipstick. In the beginning of "2016" it says: "I love you even when you don't love me, sometimes forever." It had two hearts at the end of the message and he never erased it. He was upset with me one day so I wrote that message on his mirror so when he came home he would see my apology. I'm trying to understand why GOD would have me in this bathroom doing this all by myself. I think he knows that I need to begin to handle my affairs although I was going to tell one of our sons to do it. I was in tears crying and asking GOD again why.

As I'm scrubbing away my tears are falling into the sink going down the drain, I then go to clean the shower I step inside and just continue to cry thinking of all the times my husband took a shower in here and now here I stand ALONE. Is this true story? Yes, this is a true story. I go through his things that he had scattered around and I remember one time when my husband was in the bathroom and I came inside to tell him something, he was sitting on the toilet with his headphones on he looked up at me and smiled.

I gave him a kiss on his forehead which is what I would do when he was on his "Throne" I looked around that bathroom and I said, "Husband this bathroom is a mess" then I said "you better not leave this mess for me to clean up one day." He playfully said, "Be quiet and get out" we laughed then I closed the door and went on about my day. But now I wonder why I would've ever said such a thing. Someone please tell me why would I say that because when I said it I meant in our old age, that is what I meant right?

May 6, 2017, I woke up at 6:04 am today and I almost didn't remember where I was but everything came into focus laying in my home, my room, and my bed alone no Devan. I said my prayers, did my praise and worship talked to my sister then it all started to hit me again as it does every day.

The week after my husband passed I was laying in my room our room in bed when my one of my sisters called me. Something that she said has stayed with me she told me that this will get better over time and that it will hit me in waves. I didn't understand what she was even talking about. How will it get better? This thing called grief is really real I went to the salon it's been three weeks since I've been there on a Saturday, I'm actually starting to feel a lot more comfortable being there since GOD has sent me a new team.

As soon as I stepped back from trying to figure things out

GOD began working. The more that I'm there, I'm starting to see people that have been trying to come pay their respects. I had a man walk in yesterday he says, who owns this now? Is it the same owner? I said what do you mean? He says, well didn't the guy that owned this die? I paused so I could collect my words because I'm certain that he meant no harm and he obviously didn't know that I was Devan's wife. So I said, I'm Devan's wife and unless GOD tells me to leave I'm not going anywhere. His response was "I'm sorry ma'am I didn't know, GOD bless you and your business." I guess this is to be expected I realize that some people just don't know what to say.

I need to make sure that I'm perfect for May 20, 2017 because I am accepting and award on behalf of my husband and I must represent him well. I am honored to receive this. However, I wish he could walk on that stage himself. I needed to purchase some shoes to match the beautiful gown so I decide to go to Nordstrom's. When I think about it The Holy Spirit led me right to them. I'm mean literally sat me down and I just happen to glance over and they were right in my face. PERFECT!!!!

May 7, 2017, I woke up at 6 am again; but I fell back to sleep until 9 am, talked to GOD, and currently listening to my praise and worship. In this moment, I feel sad the sun is partially shining and it's 51 degrees outside. I wonder if I am prematurely wanting to move to Tampa but then I know it's time. I would've never thought about leaving Cincinnati before now. Devan always wanted to move but I kept saying, "Husband let's wait a little longer." Well he has already moved so what purpose do I have staying in Cincinnati?

Our children are grown with their own lives and families. It's time for me to take care of myself the way GOD intended and the way my husband would if he was still *here. This book is so important for me to share with others because someone will face the loss of a spouse and they will not have any idea how they will continue on without them. I am shedding tears as I write because I am so hurt and angry right now I have cried every day since being back in Cincinnati although I do cry in Tampa it's different.*

I need to get out this house today, I've been back four days and it's starting to settle in again. I noticed an ache in my neck on the left side. It feels like a muscle strain but I haven't done anything that would cause that. I spoke with my holistic acupuncturist and she told me that emotional stress gathers in that area which relates to the grief. She also told me the left side is the female and it relates to the fact that I'm alone at the moment. The right side is the masculine side which relates to the responsibility that I have taken on. This happens whenever I come back home from Tampa.

May 8, 2017, today is the beginning of a new week and I woke up in a better space. Last Monday was very hard because it was the first Monday of the month which represents that time just keeps moving in spite of my husband being with GOD. Yesterday was a hard day as well I couldn't stay home all day. So I got out and went to my sister's house. We had a good time which we always do. He is always there for me, I realize that I am so blessed to have the people who I have in my life. I promise I don't know what I would do without them. GOD already knew how much I would need them and they often tell me, "Sis, I thought I was supposed to be here for you but honestly you have helped and changed me." All of my sisters and brothers have told me that at some point since Devan has passed away.

Wow, so you know what I say to them? Well, I guess we

need each other! They allow me to cry, scream, yell, vent, talk and JUST BE whatever I want to and if they get tired of any of it, they never show it. See GOD made sure that I would have the best foundation with me before he allowed My Devan to be called home. He removed a lot of people who I thought would be here with me. During this time away from me, my feelings were slightly hurt for a quick second but I understood why GOD did that. He handpicked my squad and the people he removed they didn't make the cut. As I look back now I am so glad I didn't go against who he has for me.

This coming Sunday is Mother's Day the very first one since my husband's passing!

~CLARITY~

I have decided as of today that after I move in the next couple of months I will stay in Cincinnati for a year then officially move to Tampa. We will see what the next year holds because GOD revealed to me that March 19, 2019, is going to be an epic day. I'm not sure what it holds but I know that it's something really amazing and I'm excited about everything that is coming my way. I've been in the house for the entire day so I decided to get a few things done in my room, I felt productive today and so far no tears. I felt kind of lonely today but I just continue to trust, GOD. Today I had no distractions at all from people or things.

May 9, 2017, Last night I went to bed watching some of our videos and it was so hard. I look at this man and I wish I could just have him back. I wish I could have just one more moment with him. When I look in the mirror at myself I just can't believe sometimes that it's just me. Of course, I woke up to rain as I laid in bed praying for Gods will today, I prayed for The Holy Spirit to give me everything that I am going to need today.

My neck is still very tight so I am wondering if I should go see my trainer this morning. I am glad I decided to go see her because my neck actually doesn't feel as tight which further lets me know that it's just tension and stress. I will make it through all of this! GOD is with me and I know that Devan is as well. I know that he sees my tears, my pain, and my strength because he always told me.

I've had a few people speaking over me since Devan passed away I only allow and receive from people who I know truly has a word from GOD and each time that it's happened it's consistent with what I've already been told *so I know its confirmation. My brother called me on Devan 6 month date of being gone and I was in a space of missing him so when he called it was right on time. He was with one of his friends who happens to be a very well-known prophet.*

We'd never met one another before so what he was about to say to me was straight from GOD. He told me that I had a youthfulness about me and my sense of humor will keep me young for many years to come, I suffered a great loss which has caused me pain, but that is over no more pain, he said death passed you over, no more that is a thing of the past, people have been wondering what you've been doing and you are about to show them what you've been doing, things had been slipping through your fingers, no more lack.

He said, "I see men catering to you and taking care of you." I see an older woman praying for you and her prayers are helping to sustain you. I see you mentoring young girls, men, women, and your name will be well-known in the City Officials office for being great. You will have a father figure enter into your life, like you've always wanted. He said, be careful of certain women because some around me are jealous. He said all of these things plus so much more. I was speechless because what he was saying was just more confirmation of what GOD has already told me.

May 11, 2017, yesterday was our Maurez birthday. He turned 24 and he had to celebrate without his daddy. I could see and feel the pain which hurts me because I can't make it better. Parents are supposed to celebrate their children birthdays with them, they are supposed to see them get married, raise their children, buy their first home, and so much more but that isn't our reality.

May 13, 2017, last night was the Relay for Life Event given by the American Cancer Society. I was invited to speak and share my story. It was amazing being a part of something so meaningful, I was very inspired as well. I thought about my husband and how he was with me through everything but now he isn't here with me in the world. It was very emotional for me and as I now sit here and look at his videos and pictures I feel very deeply saddened. I imagined him in the audience watching, smiling and cheering me on.

Just finished my day in the salon and now I'm sitting in the shop and I'm very happy with how the salon is growing because all the chairs are full and as I sit up front at my husband's station I look outside I see a couple riding a motorcycle and tears begin to fall from my eyes, it's a beautiful day and I can't help but reminisce on how we use to ride our motorcycle like that. I would be on the back of Devan's bike holding on to him, loving him that was our thing riding on the motorcycle it added to the connection we already had.

I am so sad in this moment, Where is my husband? He passed away on a beautiful Saturday like today. This is so hard it changes in the blink of an eye, one moment I am laughing then the next moment I am very sad. People say are you okay? My sisters often ask, "What just happened you were fine a second ago," My husband left that's what happened. Is this how it will be the rest of my life? Will everything remind me of my husband? Will every scent, occasion, moment pull me back to the fact that I will never see Devan again in this world?

May 14, 2017, Mother's Day is a day that I typically would spend with my husband. I would normally do something with my mom the day before. Things are very different for me and our family so my children came to get me, we went to lunch along with my mom which was special. I had fun. Afterwards, my sisters and I spent some time together, just hanging out being sisters. I was angry when I woke up. However, the day turned out to be very nice. Now, I need to get some rest because tomorrow is a big day for hair, makeup and photo shoots. I am purposely living out loud and walking through this pain.

May 18, 2017, today I woke up grateful. I didn't realize how emotional I was going to be since I've decided to sell the house. I have to allow the Realtor to list the house which means they have to take pictures. I've been putting it off and postponing this day but today it had to be done. When she walked in I immediately felt the irritation and frustration starting to set in. She went from room to room taking pictures of my house, our house, the house that I will never share with my husband again. I wanted to scream "get out of our house." I stood in the living room remembering the last time my husband and I sat in that space which was the Tuesday before he passed.

Each room she walked in brought up a memory of the last time we were in that particular space together. GOD, is this really happening? Why didn't I have my sisters here with me during this process? I had no idea that this would hurt like this and the tears won't stop flowing. It's just so much to losing your husband, it's not just they're gone and life goes on.

So I called on The Holy Spirit, Right now I need you to give me peace, courage, acceptance, understanding and right now in this moment. I know that there is purpose behind all of this and there's a reason. Just knowing that the cause of the reason is that Devan is no longer here. My heart is beating so fast GOD, please comfort me. I know for a fact that Devan would've never left me willingly. If he knew that he had to leave, he would have left me in a better position meaning he would've made sure I wouldn't have to handle things like selling our home. I just really miss my husband,

I really miss Devan.

May 18, 2017 (PM), as I sit in bed with the deck open writing it's quite in the house but I can hear the sounds of the city, I can hear the motorcycles outside, I can't help but think about Devan and I riding on nights like these. I went to workout after the lady left my home that helped me release some of the pain.

I went to the salon for a couple of hours I decided to clean out some of the things in Devan station. I thought that I would be okay because it was people there but that wasn't the case. I allow my tears to fall whenever, wherever and around whomever. I will never hold my grief inside so today was a very emotional day for me. Our three-year-old granddaughter sent me a video message asking why GOD make her paw paw go to sleep now? She wants him to wake up! So very heartbreaking to me, I never knew what it meant when people said someone died of a broken heart, but now I understand what that means. If I didn't have GOD in my life the way I do, I would be one of those people.

May 20, 2017, today is another big day I am going to prepare myself for the Gala this evening. Devan is being inducted along with six others. I have been wondering if I should write a thank you speech. I have chosen not to do that because I speak so much better from my heart and being authentic at the moment and feeling what I need to feel at "that" moment. I was talking to GOD this morning and just being so grateful and thankful because my life is so new and fresh each day.

I carry an indescribable feeling inside of me because my husband is with GOD. I have to purposely decide to get up and literally put one foot in front of the other foot all while trusting GOD. I used to open my eyes ready to roll over to my husband and say what I had a dream about but I no longer do that because I can't. I am so overjoyed because the outpour of love that I have received since my husband's passing has been amazing. I just never knew of all the love people have for us. It was not just people I know but complete strangers as well. I wake up several times in a week to uplifting and encouraging messages from people telling me that I inspire them and to never stop sharing. This encouraged me and further lets me know that I am walking in my purpose. I thank GOD for all of it.

May 21, 2017, The Gala was amazing I felt like I was at The Golden Globes it was so beautiful as I walked in my heart was beating fast and I didn't fully know what to expect. I had a wave of emotions the entire day. I was in awe at the event and in some type of trance because of the reason I was there. My Devan was going to be inducted into The Black Business Hall Of Fame.

When they began speaking about my husband and all that he/we did to deserve the award I could see Devan standing up on the stage accepting this honor. However, when I walked up and on the stage it felt like I was walking back on the stage, like I did at his service. All eyes were on me watching the widow receive this on behalf of her husband. Why do we wait to honor people after they pass away? Why can't we honor them while they can physically see and be a part of it?

I 'm a widow, yes a widow and to be honest, I'm not happy about it. There is nothing in this world that will ever change the fact that my husband is not here. My children are having a hard time today and when I think about some of the people who said they would be there for not just me but our children haven't stepped up. Frankly, it's quite a few that my children call uncle that have yet to check on them. I wish I could literally take this pain from them. I don't tell them that it will get better, I tell them to allow themselves to feel whatever it is that needs to be felt in the moment. Being a part of the Gala is only the beginning of what's in store for me that was just a taste I can see very clearly where I'm going.

May 22, 2107, my stomach is turning right now. I woke up today and I thought I heard my husband in the bathroom. I started to call out to him but then reality kicks in. Out of the 239 days, I've cried 235 of them and counting for my husband. I keep waiting for the saying, "Time makes it better" when is that and who knows that? I am just learning how to live with it and my children are learning how to live with it. My friend's father told her the other day, "Once Kim meets someone else she will forget about Devan," WHAT??!! I was appalled because he obviously doesn't know what it feels like to lose a piece of yourself, how dare he? I guess because for him that rings true but I can't even imagine ever forgetting "My Devan."

~PURPOSE BEHIND THE PAIN~

Eight months ago my life changed in the blink of my eyes my world as I knew it was forever changed and looking back I am amazed at how I have endured it all. I know that if GOD wasn't my everything that I would not be where I am in this moment. I have done so much in these past eight months than in the last two years. The woman who was, is no longer here and a piece of her left with her husband. A new and improved woman has now emerged from this pain. Let me explain who Devan Rmoni Johnson was to me.

Devan was created specifically for me; we were created for each other, he was the only person besides GOD that knew Kimberly Nicole Johnson, he was the only man who knew how to handle me, he was my knight and shining armor, he was my King, my hero, MY LOVE, my role model, my best friend, my lover, my partner in life, my Rollie, my ride or die, my confidant, and he was my world. Devan was teaching me all along because GOD already knew that this day would come, he already knew that I would only have Devan for 21 years and nothing more. I know that GOD has a reason for everything he does.

My husband has touched more people because of his passing. I've had so many people contact me saying, "Please don't stop sharing Devan and you with us," they tell me how I have inspired them and motive them in their daily life. That for me is what it's all about if all of this is to help others realize their purpose in this world and learn who GOD is and what Jesus did then that shows me that is the purpose behind the pain.

May 24, 2017, I thought I would be okay this morning because I had a hard day 2 days ago, I can always feel when my morning is going to be a hard one. I prayed to

GOD and told him that I will continue to walk in his will which is my purpose. My sister told me I was chosen for this life at birth and that Devan and I were meant to be together we are so much alike and that my purpose isn't just for me but for the masses. I thank GOD for this because for him to allow it to be so means something that maybe I don't fully understand but I receive it.

This is what I've heard GOD say to me about my life "Daughter do you fully trust me? Don't ever stop because I know the plans that I have for you and they are good when I put you together in your mother's womb it was for a purpose. I want you to keep trusting me and walking this walk. You are never alone I am with you each step that you take. I have your angels stationed around you and they go before you.

I know you miss your husband but it was time for him to come home. I gave him to you and you to him for my will and he walked in his and now it is your turn to continue to walk in yours. You will see him again and he will forever be with you because you are one and will always be. Don't ever worry about anything in this life because I AM GOD! I need no help being who I am. I am sovereign and even when I seem far away, I am never away. I got you daughter I promise I do! and more importantly I LOVE YOU! TRUST ME AND MY WILL.

May 28, 2017, I am waking up on cloud nine this morning I recorded my first podcast last night I really enjoyed it. I didn't know what to expect but it was amazing. As I look at these past eight months, it's been a whirlwind of favor on and over my life. I wake up trusting GOD'S will for it all. I didn't cry yesterday although I think, speak and feel Devan at least 22 hours of my 24 hour day. Today I will go over Stacey's house and stay overnight with one of our other sisters for the holiday. I am missing "My Devan" bad right *now. As I began to write I turned on my music and the song that came instantly reminded me of my husband. I want to talk to him right now and I want to touch him right now but I can't. I love how GOD gives me confirmation at every turn about my walk.*

When I woke I did my morning routine which as soon as I open my eyes I give GOD thanks for everything, I talk to GOD, read my daily scriptures, I then go into my praise and worship. Today the scripture was confirmation because it came from Jeremiah 1:5. "Before I formed you in the womb I knew you, before you were born I set you a part; I appointed you as a prophet to the nations." which reminds that this is my calling and purpose in life.

June 2, 2017, Praising GOD right now! GOD is so faithful to his word all he wants us to do is TRUST HIM! I had an amazing weekend my first Memorial Day without Devan but I made it through with the help of my family. Tuesday when I woke up I felt that lingering spirit of grief hanging around so I immediately went into praise and worship. I was getting ready to go see my trainer and as I walked around my room and I picked up one of Devan shirts to wear, then when I walked into my office. I looked around at all the things in our house and broke down. I asked GOD how am I supposed to condense all my home I shared with my husband into a small apartment? I fell to my knees and screamed and cried like I just heard the news for the first time that my husband had passed away. I couldn't even workout, my sister came to get me that entire day was emotional. Yet, I was experiencing some type of healing in that moment.

Later that day, I went home to rest because I had a long morning of filming the next day. I started filming a video for a project related to my book on Wednesday. It was so amazing although I had emotional moments but overall it was exciting. I am so proud of myself because like I said before if Devan was here I would still be comfortable, yet unfulfilled. I will not allow my husband's passing to be the end of him/us. The video is going to touch so many people and GOD will get the Glory from everything that I am doing in and with my life.

During the filming, I received an email saying, 'I was approved for the apartment," that I saw the Wednesday before. I just started to shout so loud I scared the people in the Shop! Hallelujah GOD...... Thursday, I had a check-up with the Plastic Surgeon that did my reconstruction and she wanted me to go see Dr. Shapiro-Wright. I had concerns about something esthetically so to be safe she wanted me to have a sonogram on the area.

For a brief moment, the enemy tried to get me to doubt what GOD has already told me over and over. I had to remember what a prophet spoke to me from The Holy Spirit back in April and one of the many amazing things he said was "Death has passed over you that is behind you and never to return." You have much to do and it's all his goodness. So I chose to believe and trust what GOD said to me. I went to have the sonogram done and the first thing Dr. Shapiro-Wright said was, "That's nothing to worry about" which I already knew but she was just confirming what GOD told me and she had no idea she was just confirming it all.

As I waited to be called back I thought back to the time I sat in that room three years ago waiting to be seen and how my life was in transition I had no idea how much it was going to change. The nurse came out and told me that I would have to wait for about 30 minutes or so because they just started a biopsy on someone. I sat and I listened to some of the woman chatting about their business. I looked around at some of them and I saw fear and worry on their *faces. So, in that moment I said a pray for them as well as myself.*

As each woman went back before me, I started to wonder if they had forgotten about me. When in that moment this woman walked out and she looks like she had been crying. I glanced then smiled at her as she smiled back she said: "You look familiar." I said so do you she said, "Kim, I'm TJ's mom" which is one of our son's friends. We hugged each other, and then she started talking about Devan saying she was sorry to hear about what happened, she asked how I've been holding up. I told her moment by moment and trusting Gods will for my life. She told me that she had to have a biopsy again and how she went through Breast cancer twice before.

I spoke GOD into her and pled the blood of Jesus over her. She than began to tell me about her husband and how they were having problems. I listened and gave her what The Holy Spirit told me to tell her. Afterwards, they called me back and I gave her my number we hugged. I left to get the sonogram done. The sonogram tech walked me to the same room I was in three years ago, and I thought about my husband. I talked to GOD in that moment and I knew I was going to hear nothing but good news. The results were good Hallelujah! So what came to me was that the visit wasn't even for me but for the woman I spoke with in that waiting area and the women that I prayed for. I don't know what GOD needed her to see in me or from me but I truly feel it was all for her.

June 10, 2017, today is Saturday. Yet again and of course, today is hard but every day is. However, this day represents the day that my husband left this world. As I laid in bed this morning trying to enjoy the view. All I thought about was my husband and how much my life has changed in the past nine months. I felt an ache inside of me that I can't seem to shake. Everyone keeps saying, "It will get better in time, Devan is with you, and you are not alone, blah blah blah!

What about right now in this moment? I feel alone, Devan isn't physically here and I know that GOD is with me. That doesn't change the facts that Devan is gone.... I didn't ask for this. I have to leave the life I had, the life me and my husband built together to start a new one. Will this grief last forever? Is it robbing me of being Kim? I wonder if people feel sorry for me when they see me out alone? Why would they? Everyone doesn't know I'm sitting here grieving my husband, no one knows that I cried my eyes out this morning, and that I'm afraid yet excited about what's next. Do I look like a widow? Do I look scared, lost, unsure, vulnerable, and lonely? What do they see when they see me?

~ JULY 1, 2017~

I will get the keys to my new place on July 1, 2017. I feel like I am burying another part of my life AGAIN! Father's Day is next Sunday and my children don't have their daddy to celebrate with, this all seems so unfair.

Have you ever been on vacation? Let's think about what vacation means. It means to relax have fun enjoy every moment. Sometimes when you go on vacation things may occur like missing luggage, flights changes, sometimes people lose things, and you may even have a disagreement with someone while on vacation. Overall, it's supposed to be fun, relaxing, restoring, life changing, it allows you to be refreshed, and rejuvenated correct?

Well guess what, this isn't our home we are on "VACATION." We must never forget that we all have a day to leave this temporary place. As I think about life, I realize this isn't our home. My husband is at home I know for certain that Devan Rmoni Johnson is in Heaven with GOD which means he's at home. So enjoy your vacation and make sure that your home will be with God once it's all over.

This journey has truly shown me so much about who I was, who I am, and the woman who I'm evolving into. It's showing me who's for me. GOD has removed, replaced, and restored people in my life. I am enjoying the journey. I am not afraid to live and I enjoy my life. I want to be an example of strength for the world. I can get overwhelmed and scared sometimes but then I call The Holy Spirit.

Losing my husband has been very hard for me but I choose to Trust GOD daily, therefore making everything else easy. I will continue to share my purpose to the world..... Stay tuned because this is only the beginning and I have so much to do and share.

To be continued……..

These are words from a few of the people who Devan touched as he soared:

Devan Johnson was truly a person that was one in a million. I never met someone who cared more about other people's well-being than he did. He loved making others feel great about themselves through fashion and grooming and would not hesitate to tell you how great God is in the process. When I first met Devan it was in Houston, TX and I thought to myself who is this happy, stylish guy running around all over the place with clippers in his hand? He came up to me and asked "Hey Cuzz, who cut your hair?" I answered "this barber in Las Vegas, why?" He told me to have a seat and after he finished I would think long and hard about going back to him.

He was absolutely right I never went back to that barber, and little did I know that day in Houston was the start of a beautiful friendship. That was the longest hair cut that I think I ever had but it was well worth my butt falling asleep in the chair when I saw the finished product. That day alone let me know that he took pride in his work and he didn't shortcut things. That was the mentality that he had with everything in his life. He took pride in being a great father, husband, barber, stylist, community leader, and most of all to me a genuine friend. He was also a very funny person. He helped me punch up jokes and was with me before I went on stage reminding me of the jokes to try that we worked on. I have so much respect for Devan and the man that he was. If you never got a chance to meet Devan you definitely missed out on meeting an angel walking the earth.

REFERENCES

--

JAY REID
www.ComedianJreid.com
www.Facebook.com/JayReidLV
www.Twitter.com/ComedianJreid
www.Youtube.com/Jreid20

Dyehouse, Karyn M. MD

Shapiro-Wright, Hilary DO

Levick, Elizabeth, MD